# The Reasons I Pray

# *The Reasons I Pray*

## Deberann Tinson

Williams and King Publishers

Copyright 2017

All rights reserved. No part of this publication may be reproduced, stored in a retrieval system, or transmitted in any way by any means electronic, mechanical, photocopy, recorded or otherwise without the prior permission of the copyright holder, except by reviewer who may quote brief passages in a review to be printed in magazine, newspaper or radio/TV announcement, as provided by USA copyright law. The author and the publisher will not be held responsible for errors within the manuscript.
ISBN:   978-0-9983663-6-4, 099-8-366366

All scripture is quoted in the King James Version unless otherwise noted.

All definitions in the English language is taken from the Miriam Webster's Dictionary unless otherwise noted.

Printed in the USA

## Dedication and Acknowledgements

This book is dedicated to my mother Rubylin Bogle, who is my best friend, and who also inspired me from my childhood on how to pray. Mom, thanks for being the example of what it means to pray it through. You didn't know you were inspiring me, as I watched you praying day and night, and seeing your prayers answered right before my eyes. Thank you, Mom. I love you for life.

To my wonderful daughter, Sashoi. You helped catapult my faith to another level. You are my inspiration, to constantly walk by faith and not by sight. Thank you for giving me my beautiful granddaughter, Naomi. You both give me the reasons to pray without ceasing.

My thanks and appreciation to Apostle and Pastor Erlene Brinson, who has been my spiritual mother, and close friend. Thank you for the time you spent, teaching and grooming me in prayer. Thanks for believing in me.

Many thanks to my best friend Latonya Woodruff, who has been more than a friend but more like a sister. Thank you, Latonya for all your love.

To my Pastors Alan Newman and First Lady Martha Newman. Thank you for believing in me, for your many words of encouragement, and wisdom that you have imparted to me. Your words are still ringing in my ears, "Finish Strong!" To all my daughters and sons in Christ, Chyna, Erica, Joi, Loni, Patricia, Janice, Juanita, Alan Jr., Eric, Elder Iric, and of course, many thanks to Mother Elenzia Johnson, who is an awesome church mother.

Thanks to all my longtime prayers partners and awesome friends Joan Williamson, Dawn Pope, Emma Terry, Merlene Knight and Ilene Salab. To my former pastor and his wife, Bishop and Addy Perkins, and Mother Velma Dennis.

To JB a wonderful friend. During my time of trials, you have proven to be more than a friend. Thank you for your encouragement. Evangelist Icena Smith and Glendon Luke who have both gone on to be with the Lord.

Thanks to my sister Paulette who helped with funding the editing process of this book. Thanks sister. I love you. Thanks to my editor and publisher, Marcia Williams. You and your team are awesome. You brought it all together.

# Table of Contents

**Chapter 1**
    Answering the Call to Pray..........1

**Chapter 2**
    Prayer ..........................................9

### *Section: Why Prayer*

**Chapter 3**
    Reasons................................... 27

**Chapter 4**
    Governmental Laws ................33

**Chapter 5**
    The Burden for Souls ..............41

**Chapter 6**
    Sexual Perversion.................... 51

## Section: Let's Do It

**Chapter 7**
Develop a Passion for Prayer .. 57

**Chapter 8**
Confession the Word of God ....... 65

**Chapter 9**
Intimacy with God....................... 97

**Chapter 10**
Praying with a Broken Heart ..... 113

**Chapter 11**
Breaking Barriers Through Prayer  127

**Chapter 12**
Be Anxious for Nothing............ 155

**Chapter 13**
Overcoming through Prayer ...... 167

**Chapter 14**
Faith Mixed with Prayer............ 195

**Chapter 15**
Delight Yourself in the Lord ..... 213

**Chapter 16**
Developing a Prayer Ministry..... 227

**Resources**......................... 243
**About the Author**......................... 247

# Preface

*The Reasons I Pray* is an inspirational prayer book of reflections about my life experiences. It was inspired by real prayer life events, including the ups and downs and challenges that arise during our spiritual journey. But most importantly, it's shows how I was victorious and overcame them all. It will guide you through the barriers we erect in our lives because of unforgiveness, bitterness, low self-esteem, pride, and fear. It will equip you with scriptures that you can directly apply to your situation to experience breakthrough in every area and begin to tap into your God-given inheritance. Yes, it is truly possible to be free from bondage and I invite you to enter in this journey of prayer and reflection.

Before we do, let me share why I decided to pen this book. After watching, with deep sorrow, so many things happen in the lives of friends, family, acquaintances and even those in the ministry, I knew it was my calling to pray. It became my life's mission, and the more I developed a relationship with God, that desire to pray became my number-one priority. Soon I began to take on the responsibility of praying for nations and spiritual leaders, especially when I started to see them falling and walking away from what God had ordained them to do. I watched as our beloved country and other surrounding countries spiral downward as they indulged in the lust of their flesh - forgetting the very principles on which they were founded. I felt not just a need, rather an intense call to take on the responsibility to pray for them. Prayer has been my first love, and will always be. I confess, I am truly fulfilled when I intercede on behalf of others.

Prayer is my foundation, and it is a command of God to all of us because it has an extraordinary impact on others. Here are a few examples:

- It saves the sinners - *Luke 18:13*.
- It reveals the will of God.
- Prayer accomplishes the impossible - *Matt. 21:22*.
- Prayer defeats the devil.
- In *Luke 22:32* it strengthens the Saints,
- It heals the sick - *James 5:13-15*.
- Prayer along with the Word increases our faith which causes us to have supernatural breakthrough.

- *Matthew 17:20* talks about the mustard seed faith that causes everything to grow and develop into wonderful things.

I can't underscore how important it is to pray. God repeated the command to do so in *Romans 12:12 and Col. 4:2*. Praying to God helps the lives of all those who believe.

It is therefore my mission to bring together the faithful and to stand in prayer with those who are in need. If you or a family member need prayer, I want you to know that the Lord will hear your request through the power of agreement. Don't hesitate to call on your prayer partner or the elders of your congregation as James exhorts.

(James 5:13-15) - Is anyone among you suffering? Then he must pray. Is anyone cheerful? He is to sing praises. Is anyone among you sick? Then he must call for the elders of the church, and they are to pray over him, anointing him with oil in the name of the Lord; and the prayer offered in faith will restore the one who is sick, and the Lord will raise him up, and *if he has committed sins, they will have forgiven him.*...

# Introduction

Prayer is the act of communicating with our deity (especially as a petition or in adoration, contrition or thanksgiving). Prayer is our direct line to heaven. It is a communication process that allows us to talk to God! He wants us to communicate with Him in the same way we do on a person-to-person phone call. Cell phones and other mobile devices have become a necessity to most people today - so much so, there are new devices frequently introduced because these are the means of communication that allow two or more people to interact, discuss, and respond to each other easily. This is simply communication.

The Greek word used for prayer is *proseuche* which is derived from the word *proskartereo*. There are several Greek words which can be translated as *prayer,* but this word refers to prayer in general. It is also the word which describes a "*place of prayer*" which means intently engaged in, constantly attending to, persist in adherence to and constantly devoted to. It denotes to "continue steadfastly in thing and give unremitting cognizance to it," which signifies unremitting attention. This definition suggests not only the constancy of which we are to pray but the effort that is needed to maintain a habit so much above nature.

The Hebrew word for prayer is *Tefilah*. It is derived from the root *per-lamed-lamed* and the word *L'Hitpalel*, meaning to judge oneself. This surprising word's origin provides insight into the purpose of Judaic prayer. The most important part of any Judaic prayer, whether it is a prayer of petition, thanksgiving, praise to God, or of confession, is the "introspection" it provides (that is the moment that we spend looking inside ourselves, seeing our role in the universe and our relationship to God).

The Yiddish word meaning pray is *davened*, which finds its origin in the same Latin root as the English word divine and emphasizes the One to whom prayer our is directed. For an observant Jew, prayer is not simply something that happens in the synagogue once a week (or even three times a day). Prayer is an integral part of their everyday life. In fact, one of the most important prayers in Judaism is called the Birkat Hamazon.

Orthodox Jews are constantly reminded of God's presence and of their relationship with God because they are continually praying to Him. Their first thought in the morning, even before they get out of bed, is a prayer thanking God for returning their souls to them. There are prayers to be recited before enjoying any material pleasure, such as eating or wearing new clothes; prayers to recite before performing any Mitzvah (commandment) such as washing hands or lighting candles; prayers to recite upon seeing anything unusual, such as a king, a rainbow, or the site of a great tragedy; prayers to recite whenever some good or bad thing happens; and prayers to recite before going to bed at night. These prayers are in addition to formal prayer services, which are performed three times a day, every weekday and additional times on Shabbat and festivals.

Jews are not just blessed because they were chosen or because the promise of God was given to them. They are blessed because they are consistent in their gratitude to Him. They take His promises and acknowledge Him in all they do. They pray thanking Him before they even open their eyes to the world. Their constant thanks to Him remains their daily focus. Each time they open the Torah, they repeat His Word back to Him, reminding Him of His covenant with them.

Additional biblical references suggest that King David and the prophet Daniel prayed three times a day.

In Psalms, David states:

*"Evening, morning and afternoon do I pray and cry, and He will hear my voice" Psalm 55:$^{17}$.*

As for Daniel:

*...his windows being open in his chamber toward Jerusalem, he knelt upon his knees three times a day, and prayed, and gave thanks before his God, as he had done before. Daniel 6:10.*

# Chapter 1

## Answering the Call to Pray

Committed prayer changes things. I used the word *committed* because it takes real commitment to remain steadfastly unmovable, abounding in the things of God, especially the call to pray. Prayer ministry is one of those least participated ministries; it is not talked about extensively, but it is one of the most effective ministries in Christendom.

Deuteronomy 30:19 - *I call heaven and earth to record this day against you that I have set before your life and death, blessing and cursing: therefore, choose life that both though and thy seed may live.*

Romans 12:2 – *And be not conformed to this world: but be ye transformed by the renewing of your mind, that ye may prove what is that good, and acceptable, and perfect will of God.*

When I first started this journey, I was rebellious by nature, I would rebel against anyone who was in authority. Fortunately, one day, I made a life-changing decision — I refused to stay that way. It was then that I told myself I would not let a generational curse dictate where I should or should not end up. I wanted to be in the position to fight the real spiritual war through prayer. Yes, the only fighting I needed to do was in spiritual warfare. I vowed then to use everything to my advantage to seek after the things of God and use the Word of God to counteract the plan of the devil.

Whenever I found myself in a constant war against the wrong things, I knew I was not being effective in the Kingdom.

This is for my brothers and sisters out there:

> *Let's get it together for the sake of the Kingdom. Let's get back on our knees like Jesus did when He went on the mountain and prayed to the Father, with sweat running down His face only seeking what He was to do next. As the angels ministered to Him, He sought His Father with tears - weeping and mourning. Saints, come on with me and push through so we can bring our nation, our children and families back to God.*

*Everything we need can be found on our knees and in the Word of God.*

Luke 18:1 - *And He spoke a parable unto them to this end, that men ought always to pray, and not to faint.*

### A. He Commands All Men to Pray
1. The passage in Luke 18 does not say that only pastors should pray, or the evangelists, or even some men, it commands **all** men.

### B. Pray Always
1. I Thessalonians. 5:17 - *pray without ceasing.*
2. Not just until we get enough to get by.
3. Not just until we feel better.
4. Prayer should be a constant effort of the believer.

### C. Pray for All Things
1. Philippians 4:6 - *Be careful about nothing, but in everything, by prayer and supplication with thanksgiving, let your requests be made known unto God.*
2. A believer should pray about everything.
3. There is nothing that concerns you which does not concern God.
4. He is even concerned with the hairs on your head.

**D. Pray for all Men**

1. I Timothy 2:1 - *I exhort therefore that supplications, prayers, intercessions, and giving of thanks, be made for all men.*
2. We are commanded not only to pray for all things, but also for ALL MEN.
3. Don't be like the man who prayed, "Lord, bless me, Mom, Sue, and John - just us four and no more." It's time to mature and put aside selfishness or self-desires and to seek God for the Kingdom.
4. Jesus clearly said in Matthew 6:33 - *But seek ye first the Kingdom of God, and His righteousness; and all these things shall be added unto you.*

As Christians living in these last days, we must see the vital need to humble ourselves before God, fervently pray, hungrily seek His face and turn wholeheartedly back to Him, otherwise there will be NO POWER in our daily walk. We need to learn what the early church discovered in Acts 1:14, 2:42-47, 4:23-33, 6:4: that there is a direct connection between prayer, submission and God's Holy Spirit infilling and empowerment. The more they prayed, the more that God did in them and through them. After praying for ten days straight, Peter preached for a mere ten minutes, and 3000 people were saved! Amazing! So, based on this example, prayer is more essential than anything we can ever do. It's what will open the pathway to God to move on our request. Once we can truly model Jesus' example of prayer, then we will begin to understand the need and importance for it. According to Oswald Chambers in his book My Utmost for His Highest, "Prayer is designed more to adjust you to God than to adjust God to you and your desires".

When we begin to **live and pray as Jesus did**, we will see God's power, His mighty hand, His blessings and victories in us, in our daily lives, our churches, our nation, and our world. Jesus started out His prayer by saying, *"Father, if You are willing, take this cup from Me; yet not My will, but Your will be done,"* (Luke 22:42).

We should be breaking out in loud cries to Him with heartfelt emotions and compassion for the Kingdom of God to be enlarged. This is one way we will see our churches grow, while expanding the Kingdom of God. This is a journey we must take. Let us not make a mistake and sit within the four corners of our sanctuaries, running with titles yet missing the true calling of Jesus Christ - that He came to seek those who are lost.

Furthermore, once we pray, we must start moving in the way the prayer is directed - *work while it is day.* Once we pray, believe and obey, then we must act in faith, so we can see what we are praying about in action. You've heard it said, *"action speaks louder than words*," so praying without working is prayer without faith.

What you must pay attention to is that Jesus did both. He taught, and He practiced what He was teaching and that resulted in the building of His Kingdom. It should be the same with prayer. Prayer warriors should be the greatest soul-winners in this century because they take the first step in receiving the instructions through prayer. It is extremely important that we begin to really open our spiritual ears and follow the instructions from the Spirit of God in order to carry out the great command of God.

Here in the United States we have, for far too long, become so dependent on our access to natural knowledge, that many Christians don't even want to put their prayer and faith into action. We are admired and respected because of our knowledge, we are even attracted to people with knowledge, but sadly we have no experiences.

I believe Jesus taught about the Kingdom for three reasons - teaching, revelation of the Word, and structure. According to Apostle Guillermo Maldonado, "Teaching is to impart knowledge or skill or to give instruction".[6] Revelation is the revealed will of God. We need the revelation of the Kingdom because the revelation of the Kingdom will give us His vision.

Finally, let's talk about the power of agreement, obedience and submission. I challenge those of you who are in some type of church organization to stop fighting with those who have authority over you, submit yourselves, and then watch the supernatural power of God move in your congregation through the power of praying together. The power of agreement is essential in our churches today. We must agree together with the Father, Son, and Holy Spirit. Lack of agreement grieves the Spirit of God, which causes us not to see the results of our prayers. I have learned this through experience - not to follow is the hard way, but instead to take the simple steps in obedience.

1 Samuel 15:22 (NLT) - *What is more pleasing to the Lord; your burnt offerings and sacrifices or your obedience to His voice? Listen! Obedience is better than sacrifice, and submission is better than offering the fat of rams.*

If we look around us, we can find all types of reasons not to obey the Word of God, but obedience is the only way we will see any fulfillment in our lives. I implore you not to go with what the world is offering you, but to be transformed by the renewing of your mind.

**Time to Ponder**

Let me ask you this question: is it possible that we have trained ourselves to expect failure? For many of us, it has been the only thing that we have ever known. Can we be trapped in mindsets? Do we fall into the trap of thinking that God can use everyone else but us? Shouldn't we have gotten past our stinking thinking by now and get to the bottom of why we are not seeing the Word of God being manifested in our lives?

We must meditate on the Word of God and spend time with the Lord in prayer for wisdom and to know Him more. When we allow the Word of God to change us, to penetrate our minds and our hearts we can have a more positive outlook.

# Chapter 2

## Why Should I Pray?

**Why Should I Pray?**

This is an excellent question. There are times when it appears that our prayers are not being heard, or we are too discouraged to pray, or we think that our prayers really don't make any difference. After all, we reason that God is sovereign and His plan is unchangeable - so what difference does it make whether we pray or not?

**To Whom Do We Pray?**

Before we can answer, "Why should I pray?" We must know to Whom we pray. There is only one supreme Creator and sovereign God. There is only one way to Him, and that is through His only Son, Jesus Christ. God, our Heavenly Father, is the only one we can be assured of who hears and answers our prayers. He is the God of amazing love, mercy, and forgiveness.

The above reasoning is an example of drawing the wrong conclusions from correct assumptions. It is a fact that God is sovereign. He is working out His plan, and all will come to the end that He has ordained. However, these truths give us more reasons to pray. Why is this so? It is because God has ordained prayer as one of the ways His perfect will is accomplished.

Questions: Why pray? What is the point of prayer when God knows the future and is already in control of everything? If we cannot change God's mind, why should we pray?

Answers: For the Christian, praying should be like breathing. It should be easier to do it than not to do it. We pray for a variety of reasons. For one thing, prayer is a form of serving God and obeying Him.

We pray because God commands us to pray, Philippians 4:6-7. Prayer is exemplified for us by Christ and the early church in Mark 1:35. If Jesus thought it was worthwhile to pray, we should also. If He needed to pray to remain in the Father's will, how much more do we need to pray?

Another reason to pray is that God intends prayer to be the means of obtaining His solutions in our situations. We pray in preparation for major decisions, to overcome demonic barriers, to gather workers for the spiritual harvest, to gain strength to overcome temptation, and to obtain the means of strengthening others spiritually.

**For What Do We Pray?**
Prayer is the key to the heart of God. Prayer is the only way to a real and personal relationship with Him.

- Pray acknowledging He is God and that you accept His gracious gift, Jesus Christ, as your Lord and Savior - Genesis 17:1, Romans 6:16-18.
- Pray confessing our sins and accepting His forgiveness - Romans 3:23-26.
- Pray that His will be done in our lives, that His Holy Spirit guides us, and that we will be filled with all that God has for us.
- Pray for (spiritual) understanding and wisdom - Proverbs 2:6-8.
- Pray with thanksgiving for all the ways He blesses us - Philippians 4:6.
- Pray when we are ill, lonely, going through trials or interceding for others - James 5:14-16
- Pray to worship Him - Psalm 95:6-7.

We come to God with our specific requests, and we have His promise that our prayers are not in vain, even if we do not receive specifically what we asked for - Matthew 6:6.

He has promised that when we ask for things that are in accordance with His will, He will grant our requests. Sometimes He delays His answers according to His wisdom and for our benefit. In these situations, we are to be diligent and persistent in prayer - Matthew 7:7. Prayer should not be our means of getting God to do our will on earth but rather as a means of getting God's will done on earth. God's wisdom far exceeds our own.

There is a significant difference between believing that God exists and worshiping Him. Praying and receiving a response would not only provide you with the reason to believe in His existence but would allow us to learn about His character. It can give us more information about who He really is. Continued prayer and asking Him to reveal Himself to you, will not only help you understand His Word, it will also teach you about His character and personality which will help in developing a relationship with Him. These experiences will enrich your relationship with Him and trust me that is far better than just reading what the Bible says *about* Him.

Why is knowing God's character important? Christians run across the same problems that atheists and skeptics do - evil in the world,

His acts of judgment on people and places, etc., yet their response should be to continue to trust in Him and worship Him. What makes the difference is that Christians know God personally through having a relationship with Him and experiences that have proven to them that He is good and trustworthy. This provides them with reasons to continue trusting Him even when they don't understand the reasons for everything He does. On the other hand, people who don't know Him personally, only have the Bible as a source of information. They've read about God, but they haven't communicated with Him.

What sort of information can we learn during prayer? First, when we get a response, then we know that there is a God who is willing and able to communicate with us. An omniscient God knows what sort of response will make sense and be convincing to each of His children individually. Receiving such a response can also serve as evidence that He knows us well enough to know how to respond to our uniqueness. Asking for help and receiving it, particularly when the help is not something that would ordinarily happen or that we could bring about on our own, is evidence of His loving character. Asking for things and not receiving them often turns out to be evidence of God's good character as well. Christians are many times relieved and thankful that a prayer *wasn't* answered. Finally, He can teach us by enabling us to realize things we hadn't realized before or allowing us to see things from a different perspective.

There is a remarkable verse found in the fifth chapter of James concerning the importance and effectiveness of true prayer. The verse is located between the admonition to pray for the sick and the example of Elijah as a model of persevering prayer. At the end of James 5:16 we read these words, *"The effectual fervent prayer of a righteous man availeth much"*. In these ten words, there is much to be learned. These words can be translated differently to emphasize the key thought of the verse.

First, it is important to understand what James means by prayer in this context. It is the Word that is used exclusively for petition or request. The emphasis lies on the need of the person to receive God's blessing.

Second, we have the promise of God that prayer is effective. James states without equivocation that it avails much (when submitted by those are righteous). He does not exactly define the meaning of this statement, but in the context, it has application to accomplish God's perfect will. The goal of the Christian should be to glorify God, and He is glorified when His will is accomplished. The application of His will for the individual person may vary, but true prayer advances His glory and brings great blessings to man.

Third, prayer is powerful. There is something dynamic in prayer. No prayer ever falls to the ground without accomplishing something. The reason for this is that God is all-powerful.

Fourth, prayer should serve as a wake-up call to us. Note that James states that it is the prayer of a righteous person that avails much in its working. This should cause us to reflect on our relationship with the Lord. We need to be Christians who are walking in fellowship with Him. In addition, it is a fervent prayer that produces much.

Often, we find that our prayers are heartless and without passion. True prayer occurs when we are convinced that it is only God who can supply us with what we need.

So why do we need to pray? It is our response to God's gracious invitation to partner with Him to carry out His great purposes. Note what Paul writes in *II Corinthians 6:1* that we are *workers together with Him*. God calls us into a partnership in doing His will. One manner by which we can enter that partnership is through prayer.

- By Him, all things are possible. Jesus tells us in Mark 10:27 (NLT), *Humanly speaking, it is impossible. But not with God. Everything is possible with God.*

- *Daniel 9:18* (NLT) says that we do not ask *because we deserve help, but because of Your mercy.* Mercy means showing favor, compassion, and kindness.
- God's ultimate demonstration of love is forgiveness of the sins that each of us have committed  He is the only God who has done this but His enemy, Satan, has sent many false gods to deceive mankind. Do not be deceived nor allow anything or anyone to take priority over the only true and living God.

There is nothing we can't pray about. There are abundant references to prayer in the Bible. The scriptures also instruct us to, pray without ceasing and in everything give thanks to the Lord.

When we choose to adopt a Kingdom attitude, we will realize that we have received many blessings for which to give God praise. There will always be a reason to praise and pray. We find intimacy with God through communicating with Him in prayer. We go to Him in faith, knowing that He hears and answers all our prayers.

## How Do We Pray?

Jesus gave His disciples what we call "The Lord's Prayer" *(Matthew 6)* as a model. In addition, Hebrews 4:14-16 (NLT) tells us that we can pray boldly - *That is why we have a great High Priest who has gone to heaven, Jesus the Son of God. Let us cling to Him and never stop trusting Him. This High Priest of ours understands our weaknesses, for He faced all the same temptations we do, yet He did not sin. So, let us come boldly to the throne of our gracious God. There we will receive His mercy, and we will find grace to help us when we need it.* Above all, pray with sincerity, honor, and humbleness before the Almighty God.

For situations in which we do not know God's will specifically, prayer is a means of discerning His will. If the Syrian woman with the demon-influenced daughter had not prayed to Christ, her daughter would not have been made whole. If the blind man outside Jericho had not called out to Christ, he would have remained blind. God said that we often go without because we do not ask. In one sense, prayer is like sharing the gospel with people. We do not know who will respond to the message of the gospel until we share it. In the same way, we will never see the results of answered prayer unless we pray.

A lack of prayer demonstrates a lack of faith and a lack of trust in God's Word. We pray to demonstrate our faith that, He will do as He has promised in His Word, blessing our lives abundantly more than we could ask or hope for - Ephesians 3:20. Prayer is our primary means of seeing God work in the lives of our fellow Christians. Therefore, may He find us often before His throne, for we have a High Priest in heaven who can identify with all that we go through.

## Why Would Prayer be Effective?

God can answer our prayers, both those that involve physical circumstances and those that involve our emotional state. I know what it is to be in need, and I know what it is to have plenty. I have learned the secret of being content in any and every situation, whether well fed or hungry, living in plenty or in want - *I can do everything through Him who gives me strength*. (Philippians 4:12-13).

God knows us completely. He knows precisely what we need, even before we ask (Matthew 6:8). His omniscience also means He knows the best way to answer our prayers, including the best way to teach us and give us reason to believe that He exists. He is willing to answer our prayers and encourages us to ask for things in prayer - *ask, and it will be given to you; seek, and you will find; knock, and the door will be opened to you. For everyone who asks receives, he who seeks finds, and to him who knocks it will be opened. Or what man is there among you who, if his son asks for bread, will he give him a stone? Or if he asks for a fish, will he give him a snake? If you, then, being evil, know how to give good gifts to your children, how much more will your Father who is in heaven give good things to those who ask Him!* (Matthew 7:7-11, NJKV).

Personally, God has answered my prayers in ways unimaginable ranging from granting me peace when I was distressed (and unable to make myself feel better) to enabling me to solve problems at work, and even in Bible study. As illustrated in His Word, God has answered many kinds of prayers Acts 4:24-31, 12:1-17, Isaiah 38:1-6, 1 Samuel 1:1-20, Nehemiah 1:1-2:8.

## Why Doesn't God Reveal Himself to me Without Me Having to Ask?

God treats each person as an individual. For some people, having Him answer their prayers and to know Him would be the most effective way for them to believe. If a person's prayer to know God is answered, it is confirmation that He heard them. They've interacted with Him and by experience they now know He will listen and respond to them. Simply receiving evidence of God without asking for it first, doesn't establish a relationship with God in the way that prayer does.

Asking God to reveal Himself is a demonstration of our desire and willingness to know Him. If we are not willing to even ask God to reveal Himself, we would most likely be unwilling to follow God no matter what evidence or revelation was provided.

**Why Would the God of the Entire Universe Listen to Me?**
Some people picture God as being constantly pestered by the prayers of millions of people and wonder why He would even listen to them. Yet even with millions around the world praying to Him, God is willing and able to respond to each one of us.

Isaiah 40:28-31 (NIV) - *Do you not know? Have you not heard? The LORD is the everlasting God, the Creator of the ends of the earth. He will not grow tired or weary, and His understanding no one can fathom. He gives strength to the weary and increases the power of the weak. Even youths grow tired and weary, and young men stumble and fall; but those who hope in the LORD will renew their strength. They will soar on wings like eagles; they will run and not grow weary, they will walk and not be faint.*

**Why Pray to an Omniscient God Who Has Already Planned What He'll Do?**
God often decides to act only after people pray. This doesn't mean that He is dependent on people praying to do what He wants, but that He chooses to respond to our prayers. If He wanted to take an

action in response to prayer, He could see to it that there would be someone who would willingly pray at the right time.

There are several examples where God acted in response to prayer versus how He would have acted differently had no one prayed. Hezekiah was healed after praying to *God.* Moses prayed for God to forgive the Israelites for their rebellion. The Ninevites repented and prayed to God and avoided destruction – Peter was miraculously freed from prison after the church prayed for him - Acts 12:1-17.

**Why Should I Pray More Than Once?**
Persistent prayer doesn't mean we should repeat the same prayer over and over like a mantra. It just means that we should be consistent about praying each day. Of course, God hears our prayers the first time we pray, but sometimes prayers can't be answered immediately. One of the main purposes of prayer is to build a relationship with Him, and the best way to do that is to speak to Him daily even if it's just saying, "Father, I still want to know You, I'm still here listening for an answer." Continually asking our Creator to reveal Himself indicates a person's commitment and willingness to give Him the benefit of the doubt believing He will respond.

## How Long do I Have to Keep Praying?

If a person truly wants to know God, I believe He will enable them to find Him before they give up completely. God works differently in each person's life. Some people's first prayer maybe when they are ready to become Christians, others pray for a long time even before coming to know God. If you feel you've prayed for a long time without getting any answers, a question to ask yourself might be, "How would I respond if God did answer me?"

## How Would I Know if it's Really God?

We can hypothesize that there's an omnipotent evil deity who occasionally answers prayers and claims to be Jehovah, Allah, etc. If that's the case, we would have no hope of finding out the Truth, just as we have no hope of proving that the world and its inhabitants weren't created last week and given fake memories. On the other hand, if Christianity is true, then God is the only God, and being both omnipotent and omniscient, He can demonstrate His existence and power.

## How Can I Trust God Without Knowing Him First?

Some prayers do require the person praying to trust God first. Prayers for wisdom require that you trust in God's wisdom and ability to distribute it to others. Prayers for miracles require that you do not doubt God's ability and that you are not simply testing God - Matthew 21:21-22. Again, for emphasis, this does not mean that unbelievers are unable to pray to God, or that they must agree to worship God without first knowing his character. All an unbeliever must do is simply ask, "God, please reveal Yourself to me."

## *Why Prayer?*

As we journey together in this book, we will gain a better understanding of what God is expecting from us, His weeping and moaning men and women.

Jeremiah 9:17-18 - *Thus said the Lord of hosts, consider you and call for the mourning women, that they may come; and send for cunning women, that they may come: And let them make haste, and take up a wailing for us, that our eyes may run down with tears, and our eyelids gush out with waters.*

Let's look at some of the reasons I pray. Ready? Let's begin.

# Chapter 3

## Governmental Leaders

Our governmental bodies, including our Presidents, Prime Ministers, Kings, Queens and all those in governmental leadership positions - they are all appointed by God.

Although people exercise their right to vote, ultimately, it is God who makes the decision. Paul's writings do not suggest that God approves of a corrupt government, ungodly officials or unjust legislation. Sometimes, though, in response to the sins of a people, or for other reasons known to God, He allows evil rulers to have authority for a period even as the Old Testament prophets prophesied in times past. Ideally, God grants the authority to serve for the good of the citizenry. How that authority is exercised will be judged on the heads of each to whom it has been given.

We have seen so many types of governmental disasters, corruption and so much violence, including innocent lives that have been prematurely wiped out. We see massacres of cultic proportion, and serial shootings with hundreds of lives lost. Some of these tragedies are outcomes tied directly to the lack of prayer for our nations and for those in authority. We have drifted away from the commands of God, and sadly we seek after the limelight instead as a priority, more so than cultivating a praying lifestyle without ceasing.

On April 20th, 1999, in the small suburban town of Littleton, Colorado, two high school seniors enacted an all-out assault on Columbine High School during the middle of the school day. The boys' plan was to kill hundreds of their peers. With guns, knives, and a bag filled with bombs, the two boys walked the hallways and began their killing spree. When the day was done, twelve students, one teacher, and the two murderers were dead, plus twenty-one more were injured.[7] The haunting question remains: why did they do it? According to John 10:10-11, *The thief cometh not, but for to steal, and to kill, and to destroy. I am come that they might have life and that they might have it more abundantly. I am the Good Shepherd: the Good Shepherd gave His life for the sheep.*

It's examples like this that point to the great need for our land to be healed. We need to see changes in the government which will result in changes in our atmosphere. Honestly, I believe that a call to prayer is the only way we will see everyone live a long, safe and productive life.

In August of 2006, I had an encounter with the Holy Spirit. In that vision, He revealed the age group of people that would die as well as what would take place with our spiritual leaders. In this vision, it was the age group of zero to fifty-eight who would die prematurely without causes, from unknown diseases, heart attacks and sudden massacres. He revealed that preachers would also die untimely - even in the pulpits. Then He said, "Pray, pray, pray!"

The commander and chief of this world is the devil and according to 1 Peter 5:8 - *he roams to and fro, seeking whom he may devour.* Thankfully, God never leaves His people in the dark.

Before the war began in Iraq, I had yet another vision. This time it was of me walking over dead bodies in Israel – they seemed to be lying everywhere. Bombs were dropping all around me and I was crying and questioning. "What is going on?" That same still, small voice whispered three times, "Pray, pray, pray."

My next encounter was three weeks before the 9-11 incidents. I dreamt that planes were falling into buildings, and people were jumping out of windows. Again, bodies were everywhere. I woke up that morning, and I called my prayer warrior friends and told them about my dream. We prayed for about an hour on the phone, and we tried making sense of it but simply could not. All we knew was that something terrible was about to take place because we had an urgency to pray about the situation.

When devastating events happen, people will remember God for that moment, but when it is all over, they tend to go right back to where they were before. There is no change, no remorse, no remembering what took place - they just go on living the way they were accustomed to.

More than ever, we need to come together as a body of believers and join forces to pray for our nation, President, senators, congress, judicial system, military forces, schools, children, families, marriages, churches and spiritual leaders. We all need to be accountable to someone or something, and it is our responsibility to fight for those in authority.

This is a spiritual war we can't afford to lose, and it is time that we stand up, fight the real enemy and stop fighting each other. It's time we cut the devil's head off and let him know he cannot and will not win.

This is our set time, dear saints, and it will not be altered. We are more than conquerors! Do not give up! We fight the good fight of faith; we fight on our knees; we cry aloud and spare not. We must lift our voices like trumpets and sound the alarm in prayer!

Ephesians 6:11-18 - *Put on the whole armor of God that ye may be able to stand against the wiles of the devil. For we wrestle not against flesh and blood, but against principalities, against powers, against the rulers of the darkness of this world, against spiritual wickedness in high places. Wherefore take unto you the whole armor of God that ye may be able to withstand in the evil days, and having done all, to stand. Stand therefore, having your loins girt about with truth, and having on the breastplate of righteousness; and your feet shod with the preparation of the gospel of peace; Above all, taking the shield of faith, wherewith ye shall be able to quench all the fiery darts of the wicked. And take the helmet of salvation, and the sword of the Spirit, which is the word of God: Praying always with all prayer and supplication in the Spirit, and watching thereunto with all perseverance and supplication for all saints.*

Our fight is *not* against each other. It is against the forces of darkness and spiritual wickedness in high places. The high place emphasizes the fact that it is not mere men we face, but the wiles of the scheming adversary, and we must never underestimate his strength. He involves hand to hand combat using trickery, cunning schemes, and strategy. This spiritual battle is not a power struggle, but a *truth* struggle. God's Word of Truth renews our mind, and determines how we think, believe and ultimately how we act and behave.

## Chapter 4

## Governmental Laws

America is no longer guided by Christian principles. Secular humanism now directs the public affairs of our nation. This philosophy denies God, Christ, and the Bible. When we remove His standards, then man is free to substitute his own standards of morality, and we disallow the divinity of Christ and His completed work on the cross. The moral compass points to what is right in the eyes of everyone without respect to God's standards. Things that once appalled us now have become commonplace. We have heard so much evil that it doesn't bother us anymore, even as Christians we have fallen prey!

Let's look at some of the laws that were presented which are contrary to God's Word.

1) Oregon approved legalized physician-assisted suicide in 1994 and reaffirmed the law in 1997, making Oregon the first government in the world to make the practice legal. [8]

2) California law AB1785 requires pro-homosexual tolerance education, including all public schools and grade levels, and AB1931 provides taxpayer-funded grants to take children on field trips to teach them diversity and tolerance of homosexuality. [9]

3) Partial-Birth Abortion Ban Act 2003 (Pub.L.108-105) – This is an "unsuccessful" federal regulation bill to prohibit the performance of "partial-birth," "dilation and extraction" (D and X) or "intact dilation and evacuation" (intact D and E) late-term abortion procedures, which entail:

> (1) delivery of the torso
> (2) piercing the undelivered skull,
> (3) collapsing the skull via suction curate,
> (4) completing delivery.

This bill was vetoed, and the override failed in the U.S. Senate. Thank God for prayers being answered. [10]

## Activist Court Decisions

Supreme Court is charged with interpreting and defending the most fundamental of our nation's laws, the U.S. Constitution. As such, inappropriate judicial action by this body adversely influences the very essence and character of America. For example, in 1962, the Supreme Court decided, without sighting any precedence, that the term "church" in "separation of church and state," would now mean the "exercise of any religious activity in public".[11] This meant that the term "separation of church and state" no longer simply involved a ban on Congress from imposing a national religion but more broadly involved a prohibition against America's citizens practicing religious activities in public. This new interpretation paved the way for other judicial actions directed at removing all forms of religion from every conceivable aspect of public life.

Has America's most fundamental founding truth been crushed into obscurity? This nation was founded to assure its citizens *freedom of religion, NOT freedom from religion!*


## Decisions already rendered have resulted in:

1. **Removal of student prayer:** "Prayer in its public-school system breaches the constitutional wall of separation between church and state."

2. **Removal of Bible readings:** June 17, 1963, "No state law or school board may require that passages from the Bible be read or that the Lord's Prayer is recited in public schools at the beginning of each school day." The court went on to say, "[If] portions of the New Testament were read without explanation, they could be psychologically harmful to the [student]. [12]

3. **Removal of the Ten Commandments from view:** "If the posted copies of the Ten Commandments are to have any effects at all, it will be to induce the school children to read, meditate upon, perhaps to venerate and obey, the Commandments. This is not a permissible state objective under the Establishment Clause. [13]

The nation that rejects God accepts unnatural affections as normal. Romans 1:26-27 - *For this because God gave them up unto vile affections: for even their women did change the natural use into that which is against nature: And likewise, also the men, leaving the natural use of the woman, bound in their lust one toward another; men with men working that which is unseemly, and receiving in themselves that recompense of their error which was meet.*

The nation that rejects God becomes a nation of fools. Romans 1:21-22 - *Because that, when they knew God, they glorified Him not as God, neither were thankful; but became vain in their imaginations, and their foolish heart was darkened, professing themselves to be wise, they became fools.*

Let's look at Israel's idolatry and see the similarities our beloved country is following.

"Sacred prostitution" was common among Canaanite religions. At first, it has been just immoral sex, but soon they were involved in idol worship. Before long they were in over their heads, absorbed into the practices of the pagan culture. **Their desire for fun and pleasure caused them to forget their spiritual commitment and their moral standards. It sounds just like people in today's world! People relax their standards; compromise their morals to justify their desires.**

This combination of sexual sin and idolatry was Balaam's idea Num.31:16, Rev. 2:14, the same Balaam, who had just blessed Israel and who appeared to be on their side. It is easy to see how the Israelites were misled, for Balaam seemed to say and do all the right things - much like preachers and teachers today. Not until Balaam had inflicted great damage on them did Israel realize that he was greedy, used sorcery, and was deeply involved in pagan religious practices.

We must be extremely careful to weigh both the words and the deeds of those who claim to offer spiritual help. Baal was the most popular god in Canaan, the land Israel was about to enter. This "god" was represented by a bull, a symbol of strength and fertility. He was the god of the rains and harvest. The Israelites were continually attracted to Baal worship, in which prostitution played a large part, throughout their years in Canaan. Because Baal was so popular, his name was often used as a generic title for all the local gods. Numbers 25:1-5 - *And Israel abode in Shittim, and the people began to commit whoredom with the daughters of Moab. And they called the people unto the sacrifices of their gods: and the people did eat, and bowed down to their gods. And Israel joined himself unto Baal-peor: and the anger of the Lord was kindled against Israel. And the Lord said unto Moses, take all the heads of the people, and hang them up before the Lord against the sun, that the fierce anger of the Lord may be turned away from Israel. And Moses said unto the judges of Israel, slay ye, everyone, his men that were joined unto Baal-peor.*

Exodus 20:3-5 - *Thou shalt have no other gods before Me. Thou shalt not make unto thee any graven image or any likeness of anything that is in heaven above, or that is in the earth beneath, or that is in the water under the earth: Thou shalt not bow down thyself to them, nor serve them: for I the Lord thy God am a jealous God, visiting the iniquity of the fathers upon the children unto the third and fourth generation of them that hate Me.*

Exodus 20:23 - *Ye shall not make with Me gods of silver, neither shall ye make unto you gods of gold.*

Exodus 24:3 - *And Moses came and told the people all the words of the Lord, and all the judgments: and all the people answered with one voice, and said, all the words which the Lord hath said will we do.*

We must stay on the wall - die to ourselves, fight for the lives of others, for our nation, for our family, for our children, for our churches, for our government, and for the world.

There are several scriptures that explain the duty of a watchman on the wall. Ezekiel 3:17-19 - *Son of Man, I have made you a watchman for the people of Israel; so, hear the word I speak and give them warning from Me. When I say to a wicked person, 'You will surely die,' and you do not warn them or speak out to dissuade them from their evil ways to save their life, that wicked person will die for their sins, and I will hold you accountable for their blood. But if you do warn the wicked person and they do not turn from their wickedness or from their evil ways, they will die for their sin; but you will have saved yourself.*

Isaiah 62:6 - *I have set watchmen upon thy walls, O Jerusalem, which shall never hold their peace day nor night: ye that make mention of the LORD, keep not silence.*

This is not the time to be silent, sit back and relax. The prophet had the duty to deliver the sobering message: unless the citizens of Israel and Judah acknowledged their sins, turned from them, repented and began to obey God's law once again, they would die in their sins.

Regardless of how individuals responded to the warning, if they heard the message, the prophet did his job and was no longer responsible. Only if the prophet did not deliver the admonition would he be judged according to the scriptures.

A part of the prophet's message was showing the people how to live and maintain their faith. It was not just a bellowing message focused only on pointing out their problems. If the goal is to get people to turn back to the Word of God, then the message must also show the benefits of doing so. It must show the positive, better way of life God desires His people to live.

## Chapter 5

## The Burden for Souls

*Proverbs 11:30: The fruit of the righteous is a tree of life; and he that winneth souls is wise.*

The greatest wisdom in the world is shown by the humble soul winner. The Savior Himself indicated that one soul is worth more than the entire world. Mark 8:36-38 - *For what shall it profit a man, if he shall gain the whole world, and lose his own soul? Or what shall a man give in exchange for his soul? Whosoever, therefore, shall be ashamed of Me and of My words in this adulterous and sinful generation; of him also shall the Son of Man be ashamed, when he cometh in the glory of His Father with the holy angels.*

The Bible teaches that Hell is a definite place in such passages as Luke 16:19-31 and Revelation 20:10-15. There are many programs and activities in churches to help people, but none of them come close to being as important as soul winning. Only soul winning can keep sinners out of the torments of eternal fire. The Apostle Peter said that Christ lived "as an example, that ye should follow his steps".

No matter what, we must suffer to win souls. We cannot honestly say we are following Christ unless we make soul-winning a top priority. This was His primary business, and He did it at a great cost and suffering. It is wise to follow the example of Christ at any cost. Think of the rewards you will receive right here on this earth and in eternity for winning souls. The man who works night and day until his youth is gone focused on acquiring a fortune, may wake up to find his fortune gone overnight. Even if he can hold it in the clutches of his withered hands, death will finally drag him away, and his riches will slip from his trembling fingers. Men do not carry their wealth into the grave!

The fame of this world is hard to win and easy to lose. On his election to a second term, President Nixon won by the most overwhelming vote the nation had ever seen.[14] Yet a few months later, he was driven out of office by his enemies and had to go into virtual exile for years.

We must learn to hear the voice of the Lord. On two occasions, the Lord spoke to Philip in Acts 8:26, 29. We must learn to tune our spiritual ears to His voice. John 10:27 says, "*My sheep hear my voice, and I know them, and they follow Me".* We hear so many voices and are influenced in so many ways in the course of the day that we must take the time to study the Word, have prayer, meditation, and fast. These will allow us to understand the voice of God and tune our frequency to His so that we don't miss crucial opportunities.

## Spiritual Leaders

Those in authority are human, and they are subject to the same type of spiritual adversaries we face on a day-to-day basis. Galatians 6:1 - *Brothers, if someone is caught in a sin, you who are spiritual should restore him gently. But watch yourself, or you also may be tempted.*

Christians shouldn't commit sin deliberately. We are sometimes overtaken by sudden temptation or urged by impetuous or headstrong passion. The Apostle Paul in the book of Galatians was evidently referring to those who had fallen into some sensual indulgence, as he continued in the previous scripture.

It is a very important qualification for those who would recover others from sin that they should not be guilty of the same sin themselves. Reformers should be holy persons; people who exercise discipline in the church and in the truth of the Word.

They should be "spiritual" men and women - people in whom implicit confidence may be properly reposed.

We are called to pray without ceasing, meaning our spiritual eyes should be sharp and open to see the cunning plays of the enemy, and to keep praying for our spiritual leaders. I am seeing more and more that there are no individuals spiritually covering these men and women of God - their backs are exposed and left wide open for the enemy to have a field day with them. Let us not sit by and point fingers at them when we should be praying for them.

> *Considering thyself, remembering how liable you are to err; and how much kindness and indulgence should, therefore, be shown to others* (Matthew Henry Commentary).[15]

God has given me a special mandate to lay in the gap for spiritual leaders all over the world. There are times when the Holy Spirit will give me the unction to fast and pray for certain individuals and I have had the opportunity to see the results. Some of them were fully restored able to shake the dust off their feet and keep moving, while others had to take their time through the restoration process. I've seen the awesome results of praying and fasting and I know without a doubt that prayer does indeed change things.

There is power in consistent praying, and it's the reason why I pray.

**Marriages**

Marriage was instituted by God as a lifelong commitment, (Genesis 2:18-24, Matthew 19:3-6), in fact during the Old Testament period, everyone was expected to be married and have children. Despite this, Jesus was unmarried and said remaining unmarried (celibacy) was an excellent choice for those who could accept that life and devote themselves to God. The Apostle Paul was also unmarried. He said remaining unmarried, was a good and holy alternative, but it was better to marry than to be tempted into immorality by passion, (1 Corinthians 7:8-9). Peter and many of the other apostles were married (Matthew 8:14), so marriage is compatible with committed service to God.

Divorce, on the other hand, is a genuine tragedy. It often leaves the marriage partners embittered and disillusioned. It robs the children of the love and security of a healthy family and denies them a good role model for their own future marriages. We need to try each day to keep our marriages strong and not let them drift toward divorce. We must put aside our anger, forgive our spouse a million times over, always be faithful, do away with our pride and ego, and always, always let love to guide our actions.

According to the Old Testament Law, a man could divorce his wife if he found something indecent about her (Deuteronomy 24:1-4), but wives did not have the same privilege. Jesus saw the injustice and pain of divorce and said that neither husband nor wife should separate from the other. Jesus also said that remarriage after divorce constitutes adultery: Matthew 19:3-9 - *Some Pharisees came to Him, and to test Him they asked, is it lawful for a man to divorce his wife for any cause? He answered, have you not read that the one who made them at the beginning 'made them male and female,' and said, 'For this reason, a man shall leave his father and mother and be joined to his wife, and the two shall become one flesh?' So, they are no longer two, but one flesh. Therefore, what God has joined together, let no one separate. They said to Him, why then did Moses command us to give a certificate of dismissal and to divorce her? He said to them, it was because you were so hard-hearted that Moses allowed you to divorce your wives, but from the beginning, it was not so. And I say to you, whoever divorces his wife, except for unchastity, and marry commits adultery.*

The word translated here as "unchastity" was *porneia* in the original Greek Bible text. It means illicit sexual intercourse, including adultery, incest, etc.[16] Only *Matthew* mentions *porneia* as grounds for divorce. The references to divorce in *Mark* and *Luke,* showed that Jesus did not allow this exception.

Saints, the institution of Marriage is being assaulted daily so as prayer warriors, let us take a stand, cry aloud and spare not. Lift your voice, sound the alarm, decree and declare war against the enemy that comes to destroy family relationships. Pray that these relationships be restored back to their rightful place. We have a solemn responsibility to uphold the sanctity of marriage and the moral fabric of our beloved country.

Marriage is like Christ and the Church. Ephesians 5:22-31 - *Wives, be subject to your own husbands, as to the Lord. For the husband is the head of the wife, as Christ also is the head of the church, He Himself being the Savior of the body. But as the church is subject to Christ, so also the wives ought to be to their husbands in everything. Husbands, love your wives, just as Christ also loved the church and gave Himself up for her, so that He might sanctify her, having cleansed her by the washing of water with the word, that He might present to Himself the church in all her glory, having no spot or wrinkle or any such thing; but that she would be holy and blameless. So, husbands ought also to love their own wives as their own bodies. He who loves his own wife loves himself; for no one ever hated his own flesh, but nourishes and cherishes it, just* as Christ also does the church, because we are members of His body.

Genesis 2:24 – *For this reason, a man shall leave his father and mother and shall be joined to his wife, and the two shall become one flesh.*

## Suicide

Suicide is the act of intentionally causing one's own death. It is often committed out of despair, the cause of which is frequently attributed to a mental disorder such as depression, bipolar disorder, schizophrenia, borderline personality disorder, alcoholism, or drug abuse.[17] Stress factors such as financial difficulties or troubles with interpersonal relationships often play a role. Look at the following statistics:

### The U.S. Suicide Statistics Emergency Room Visits[18]

**Emergency room visits for self-inflicted injury: 400,000**

| | | | |
|---|---|---|---|
| All suicides | 30,622 deaths | per | 100,000 of population |
| Firearm Suicides | 16,869 deaths | per | 100,000 of population |
| Suffocation Suicides | 6,198 deaths | per | 100,000 of population |
| Poisoning Suicides | 5,191 Deaths | per | 100,000 of population |

This chart sums up the three most common methods of suicide. Note that firearms are by far, the most common method for suicide, thus, it is imperative that a suicidal person should not have access to a firearm. Hanging or suffocation is used in about one out of five suicides, which is why you can never leave an acutely suicidal person alone for a second. People who have died by hanging have used virtually every conceivable thing to hang themselves, including shoelaces, electric cords, belts, bed sheets, etc. Poisoning accounts for slightly less than one out of five suicides.

Looking at these statistics, it is evident that it is time to pray. The number of suicides is much greater now than previous years and will continue to grow. This is spiritual warfare, and it is time to fight. This battle is not for wimps, the faithless, the fearful, liars or gossipers, but it is for those that are armed with the whole armor of God.

*The Reasons I Pray*

## Chapter 6

### Sexual Perversion

Definition: Sexual perversions are conditions in which sexual excitement or orgasm is associated with acts or imagery that are considered unusual within the culture.

To avoid problems associated with the stigmatization of labels, the neutral term *paraphilia*, derived from Greek roots meaning "alongside of" and "love," is used to describe what used to be called sexual perversions. A paraphilia is a condition in which a person's sexual arousal and gratification depend on a fantasy theme of an unusual situation or object that becomes the principal focus of sexual behavior.

What does the Bible say about these actions? There are skeptics who say that the Bible does not condemn unnatural affection and there is nothing wrong with it. Various scriptures are misquoted and cause people to misunderstand the Word of God. The world wants to change God's Words and meanings into something more suitable to its sinful desires. But nevertheless, you and I know that the truth stands every time.

We should pray for the salvation of every person who continues in these iniquities. They are made in the image of God even though they're in grave sin. Therefore, we should show them the same dignity as anyone else with whom you come into contact. However, this does not mean that you approve of their behavior. Don't compromise your witness for a socially acceptable opinion.

We are living in times where the world is trying to change the standards and moral commandments that were set down by God thousands of years ago. But God is holy, just, does not change, and neither will His standards for us change or be shaped by the so-called progressiveness of this sinful world. So, the question becomes, who will you obey? Whose standards will you follow, God's or this world?

The scriptures warn that we do not to believe when the world tells us that sex outside of marriage is ok if you are practicing safe sex. The same holds true for same-sex unions with the growing tendency now to accept them as the same status as male and female marriages. God's Word warns us not to fall for these man-made standards of living.

Ephesians 5:6, 8, 11 - *Let no man deceive you with vain words: for because of these things cometh the wrath of God upon the children of disobedience. Be not yet, therefore, partakers with them... For ye were sometimes darkness, but now are ye light in the Lord: walk as children of light. And have no fellowship with the unfruitful works of darkness, but rather reprove them.*

The most common signs of sexual activity that can be classified as paraphilia include the inability to resist an impulse for the sexual act, the requirement of participation by non-consenting or under-aged individuals, legal consequences resulting from sexual dysfunction, and interference with normal social relationships. Paraphilia includes fantasies, behaviors, and/or urges which: involve nonhuman sexual objects such as shoes or undergarments, require the suffering or humiliation of oneself or a partner which can involve children or other nonconsenting partners. The most common paraphilia is exhibitionism, or exposure of the genitals fetishism or the focus on prepubescent children, sexual masochism - the receiving of humiliation or suffering sexual sadism or the inflicting of humiliation or suffering.[19]

In my research, I discovered a website called *Go Ask Alice*, created by Columbia University and recommended to children by the American Library Association.[20] This is where kids can go to find out such information as how to wash the blood off their cat-of-nine-tails after engaging in sadomasochistic sex! The poison has seeped so far into the culture that the Tucson campus of the University of Arizona was welcoming pimps, prostitutes, porn stars and exotic dancers into their classrooms to talk with students about "careers" as sex workers,[21] and to demonstrate that they too can work their way through school as a lap dancer, stripper, "escort" or actor in pornographic films. It's time to pray.

I have only identified a few reasons to pray, but of course there are, millions more. The next couple of chapters will help you to develop a passion for prayer, whether on a personal level or as a ministry.

## *Let's Do It!*

Let's buckle down and get our prayer life into gear! There are so many reasons why we all really need to take this initiative – from personal (family, finances, career), to standing in the gap for our leaders and our country.

## Chapter 7

### Developing a Passion for Prayer

*Proverbs 19:2 - It is not good to have zeal without knowledge, nor to be hasty and miss the way.*

**What is at the Root of Passionate Prayer?**

Passion in prayer needs to grow out of knowledge (both head and heart knowledge) of who God is (His character), and that He is fully capable of answering our prayers.

**What Passionate Prayer is not?**

Passionate prayer is not emotionally driven. Although emotion may be present, passion in prayer is not merely an emotional expression nor does it flow from feelings alone. Some personalities are more feelings-based than others while you may have someone else who shows no form of emotions at all. Just because someone doesn't emote in their prayers doesn't mean they aren't passionate. Try to avoid judging people based on their emotional expression. Passionate prayer is not always impressive especially when you are targeting a certain goal. High-sounding spiritual words or rhetoric may not be a part of this kind of prayer therefore, someone who doesn't know the Christian jargon can still engage in passionate prayer.

**Prayer must be a Permanent Practice**

*Pray without ceasing (1 Thessalonians 5:17)*

Let prayer become a lifestyle. To pray without ceasing is to pray all the time and for all things. We must set aside times devoted to concentrated, undistracted prayer in our individual lives. Pray without ceasing is called "practicing the presence of God" - always conscious of His presence, turning to Him as a constant companion, making no topic off limits with Him.

**Prayer Must be Consistent in Results and in Power**

The Greek seems to point to two aspects of power: one is the energy put forth in praying, and the other is the effect of those prayers.

What gives us power in prayer is that we make our petition in the authority of Jesus Christ. Even the righteousness referenced in this verse is that of Christ. The scriptures are clear that no one is righteous in oneself *(Romans 3:10-12)*. Praying "in Jesus' name" means more than tacking the phrase on to the end. When we pray in Jesus' name, we are claiming His identity, His righteousness, and His authority. Therefore this kind of prayer can't help but to have power.

The results are powerful in the sense that something will happen. Be careful not to be discouraged or disillusioned if the results are not manifested immediately or answered in ways that are out of the norm. God answers prayers with peace, wisdom, grace, and power. The peace that passes all understanding. Power to make it through the tough times and to be Christ-like in this dark and sinful world. Wisdom to apply understanding and to know what to do. Then finally, grace to overcome.

Prayer is powerful because God is powerful. As the Almighty, Omnipotent God, He does have the ability to do what we ask. As the Sovereign Lord of all creation, He has the authority to do what He knows is best in every situation. One way to emphasize the power source is to begin times of prayer with praise and thanksgiving, acknowledging His Lordship and might.

## Passionate Prayer includes:

- Devotion to prayer: Acts 2:42
- Being faithful and diligent: Romans 12:12
- Make a commitment; make it a priority: Luke 18:1
- Attentiveness in prayer: Colossians 4:2
- Be alert, watchful, clear-minded, self-controlled: Ephesians 6:18; Colossians 4:2
- Persistence in prayer; never giving up: 1 Thessalonians 5:17; Matthew 7:7; Psalm 55:16-17
- Fervent in prayer - being zealous, having enthusiasm or being energetic: James 5:16
- A Spirit-propelled effort to prayer or walking in the Spirit Ephesians 6:18; Romans 8:26-27
- A wholehearted attitude toward prayer: *Jeremiah 29:12-13*
- Seeking and loving Him with all your heart: Matthew 22:37
- A faith-driven expectancy in prayer: *Colossians* 4:2
- Being thankful before getting an answer: Mark 11:24
- A purpose in prayer, lining up with His will: Matthew 6:7-13; 1 John 5:14

## Passionate Prayer also consists of:

### Development of Faith which is:

- Knowledge of *how* He works (His will). He cares about us. Our good is at the core of His love for us and will affect how He answers our prayers.

•

### Development of Perspective which is:

- Having knowledge and understanding of *what* He says (His Word).
- Knowing that God will always be consistent with His Word in the way He responds to prayer.

Passion for prayer evolves when there becomes an increased appetite to pray more and more, which is usually the reaction when enjoying the presence of God becomes habitual and witnessing the hand of God perform miracles. Passion increases when:

**(1) Prayer is used as a means of staying focused on God.** We come to Him from a position of inadequacy, realizing that our prayers are not the power source, but He is. The way prayer works isn't always easy to figure out. We don't want to get more hung up on the activity of prayer than on God Himself. We often think that if we just pray hard enough, or long enough, or persistently enough, then things will just happen. Our prayers don't bring revival, God does.

**(2) Prayer is used as a means of acknowledging His grace.** We come to Him from a position of dependence, realizing that if anything is going to happen, it must to be because of His grace. God doesn't owe us a thing! Our prayers should acknowledge this. If our good deeds were good enough to move Him, then Jesus wouldn't have had to die for us. We should never approach the throne of grace solely on what Jesus has done for us. Isn't a pure life important? Sure, but even that is because of God's grace, so it still doesn't give us the edge in praying *(Titus 2:11-12)*.

**(3) Prayer should be a means of keeping His sovereignty in place**. We come to Him from a position of humility and submission, realizing that it needs to be His will and not our will that must be done. How easy it is to get disappointed when our prayers don't get answered the way we think they should. We somehow forget that His ways are higher than our ways *(Isaiah 55:9)*. Doesn't God promise to answer when we pray His will? Sure, but let Him be the judge of what is His will.

**(4) Prayer should be used as a means of maintaining relationship with God.** We come to Him from a position of sonship, realizing that He greatly delights in the fact that we seek Him out and come to Him. We should come to Him in prayer not primarily because we have an agenda, but because we want to be with Him, and be in His presence. Here is a tip gain to God's attention - tell Him how wonderful He is, talk things over with Him and listen to what He says. It is important to have the right motivations when praying. Like Paul; in *Philippians 3:10 - Knowing Christ and the power of His resurrection and the fellowship of His sufferings.*

## Chapter 8

### Confessing the Word of God

What is Confession? The Latin root word of confession is *confiteor*, which means to acknowledge a sin or fault, or sometimes more broadly, to simply acknowledge or vow.[22] According to Webster's Dictionary, confession is to tell or make known (as something wrong or damaging to oneself); it is to acknowledge (sin) to God or to a priest and to declare faith in or adherence to. It is also to disclose one's faults; specifically: to unburden one's sins or the state of one's conscience to God.

In this way, we might have sinners who confess their sins or believers who confess their faith. A confession might occur privately or publicly but either way, it is a necessary spoken action. For one thing, it is normal for there to be an authority to hear the confession. They may or may not have the authorization to absolve the person, but it's not really a confession if it is made alone. Secondly, a primary reason for making a confession is to help reintegrate the person back into the community or back in right standing with God. Because of the communal aspects of the act of confession, it's only to be expected that it would typically involve a ritual as well. Confessions are hardly ever just blurted out in an unstructured way. There are usually specific phrases used, both by one making the confession and one hearing it.

Daniel 9:20 - *And while I was speaking, and praying, and confessing my sin and the sin of my people Israel, and presenting my supplication before the LORD my God for the holy mountain of my God.* Daniel, though so holy and a good man, who was not without sin, thought it was his duty to confess not only his sins before the Lord, but also the sin of the people. This is the way to succeed with the Lord and experience the application of His pardoning grace and the enjoyment of other mercies and blessings. As a result, an answer was immediately sent to Daniel's prayer, and it was a very memorable one. We cannot now expect that God should send answers to our prayers by angels, but if we pray with fervency for that which God has promised, we may by faith take the promise as an immediate answer. *For He is faithful that has promised;* Hebrews 10:23. Daniel had a far greater and more glorious redemption revealed to him, which God would work out for His church in the latter days.

There was a time when un-forgiveness was a huge barrier in my life, but through confessing the Word daily over my life, it allowed God to make a complete transformation in me.

I grew up in an abusive home where my father constantly belittled my mom and physically abused her all the time. This abuse went on for years until I became very hardened, and I developed hatred for my father. I remember my sister and I would plan how we would kill him while he was asleep (we were at a tender age). We were going to light the bed on fire and burn him up. It was very difficult for us as children to watch this type of abuse day in and day out. As time went on, God brought a great deliverance to my mom that would allow her to leave, nevertheless, that was just the beginning of my problems.

I had built an internal wall that not even the strongest of iron could break through it. Hatred, resentment, and un-forgiveness seemed to be my focus, and nothing else mattered - I was a slave to these strongholds. I was saved and going to church, but no one could see my internal agony. I could not even talk nicely to my daughter or my husband at the time. If he would raise his voice a little, I was ready to charge and fight! I would yell the entire time - just mean like Hades. Unloved, untouchable, unreachable - I was just plain hateful. Every time I saw a man, and if he said one word I did not like, I would develop such a hate. It was seemingly unbreakable.

As time went on, I became disgusted with myself and could not pinpoint what was going with me. I decided to cry out to God, and immediately I heard this still small voice in my heart saying, *"That if thou shalt confess with thy mouth the Lord Jesus, and shalt believe in thine heart that God hath raised Him from the dead, thou shalt be saved."* I realized that was *Romans 10:9,* so my response to this voice was that I was already saved. And the voice responded, "Confess with thy mouth!" I decided to obey and follow the instruction that was given. Then the Spirit of the Lord told me to look in the mirror and tell Him what I saw. When I did, I did not like what I saw looking back at me.

I saw something so demonic, evil looking I could not believe I was looking at myself. It was truly as if I was looking at another person. That day, what I saw in that mirror changed my life completely. I fell to the floor, curled up in the fetal position and began to cry out in agony. I confessed everything I was and even what I wasn't. Immediately, I literally saw the hands of God forming me and making me over again in His likeness. When I came to myself, I was like a brand-new person. I had spent almost two hours before God. I immediately went back and looked in the mirror, and when I beheld the new me, there was a glow around me like a halo. I could not explain it, so I stayed in for the rest of that day and rested quietly before God.

Obedience to the call to pray changed me. I realized I did not have to rebel against the Spirit of God any longer. I only needed to rebel against the devil and allow my flesh to come into subjection. That day, prayer was birthed in me, and that hunger is still the same today.

About a week later after this encounter with God, I heard His voice again. It was a call I would never forget. I heard a still small voice say, "Meet me at 5:00 a.m. and I will show you what I will do for you." I was newly saved and still did not understand a lot of things concerning the call of God, but I knew this voice was different from what I was accustomed to. I heeded to that voice, and I got up at 5:00 a.m. every morning. My niece was living with me at the time, and I started to attend The Upper Room Prayer every Saturday morning with the International Prayer Ministry. During this time, I did not understand the beckoning to pray at 5:00 am nor the draw to this particular ministry. Coming from such a traditional church background, this was very interesting and very different from what I was accustomed. Even though I attended this early morning prayer on Saturdays, God was saying to me, "I want one-on-one time with you."

I was not filled with the gift of the Holy Ghost at the time but I had several dreams of me speaking in tongues. All I knew was, "Thank you, Jesus," and that's all I said for a very long time. By the fifth week of meeting with Him, something changed. My tongue started to go in a way I did not understand, and I could not control it. I fought to try and change it but the Spirit of God was so strong within me, that my tongue seemed to have a mind of its own. I stammered for maybe about ten minutes, but after I released my spirit to God, I spoke in tongues for more than an hour. It was at that time I understood how the disciples felt on the day of Pentecost.

I heard the voice of the Holy Spirit clearly that morning as He whispered, "I will teach you how to pray, and it will become your life." I met faithfully with Him every morning at the same time. I was consistent, and He would give me scriptures to read. I followed Him as closely as possible, not veering off course. I gleaned from every instruction as much as I could. It was then that I began to learn about moaning and groanings during fervent prayer time - still not totally understanding all these new experiences. Fortunately, my spirit knew I had a heavenly connection. It was just what the prophet said, Jeremiah 20:9 (NIV): *But if I say, "I will not mention Him or speak any more in His name," His Word is in my heart like a fire, a fire shut up in my bones. I am weary of holding it in; indeed, I cannot.*

As I continued meeting with the Lord at 5:00 a.m. I remembered asking the Holy Spirit to help me understand the interpretation of what I was saying. Suddenly the supernatural power of God overshadowed me and as I spoke in unknown tongues, I began to hear in my spirit the words in English. It went on for a long time until my understanding became fruitful. Then it was time to move onto something else as instructed by the Holy Spirit. These are the instructions given to me by the Him. *"You must ask, and it shall be given to thee. Make your request known unto to Me, and I will give you the desires of your heart."*

Immediately I went looking in the Bible for the scripture that the Holy Spirit spoke. I had to use my concordance to find it. I finally found it in Matthew 7:7-8 (NASB): *Ask, and it will be given to you; seek, and you will find; knock, and it will be opened to you. For everyone who asks receives, and he who seeks finds, and to him who knocks it will be opened.*

According to the Miriam Webster Dictionary, the word "seek" means to go after. Don't just say it would be nice to have God as your Lord, to rule your life, to be the King of your life and control your life - you must pursue it with all your heart. Seek to let God have absolute rule and control over your life. I was afraid to make an absolute surrender for fear of what God may ask me to do. I continued to search for the next phrase and found Philippians 4:6

(NASB): *Be anxious for nothing, but in everything by prayer and supplication with thanksgiving let your requests be made known to God.* I laughed out loud and responded, "I am not anxious for anything." I continued looking up my last clue and found Psalm 37:4 *(NKJV): Delight yourself also in the Lord, and He shall give you the desires of your heart.* At that point I was even more excited because I realized I had tapped into something much greater than I anticipated. Additionally, I was also learning how to pray more effectively.

One morning, I got up and opened the Bible to Psalms 75 and Psalms 45. This time I found myself praying the words as I read them. Suddenly something started to happen. I would sing and pray the Word, then cry and talk. What an awesome time! Almost immediately that still small voice spoke to me again saying, "Did you not know that your heart is desiring much more than what you already have, and your petition came up before Me?" Then He said, "Confess the Word daily." I had no idea what confessing the Word meant. So, to the best of my knowledge, I just kept praying the same scriptures all the time, even adding Matthew 6:8-13 and Psalm 23:1-6.

I fell in love with the Holy Spirit. I was so in love, that prayer began to consume me, and a deeper hunger was burning in me. I would pray in the shower, in the car and all the time around the clock. To someone standing or sitting nearby I would be talking to myself all the time - but I knew I was not crazy, I was talking to the Lord. The Spirit of God would drop in my spirit daily what or for who I needed to pray.

I developed a passion for praying for spiritual leaders and their countries. While praying for those that the Holy Spirit had put on my heart, I would begin to see international and local changes and events which would confirm that my prayers were being answered. I just could not believe what was going on but kept on as the Spirit gave me the utterance.

The Saturday morning prayer group was very instrumental to developing my true potential. Evangelist Erlene Brinson decided to take me under her wing. She is a dynamic woman of God who moves strongly in the prophetic and is such an awesome prayer warrior. I stuck to her like glue and learned everything I could.

She was the President of the International Prayer Connection and the Malone Bible Institute. She invested a lot of time and teaching in me and even paid my tuition to attend the Bible Institute for a three-year program. This was an investment well spent. I learned at that time that God is really an exceeding, exciting and abundant God.

During that time, I continued to increase in the Lord growing in wisdom, knowledge, and understanding of the Word. I had just received employment at a hotel as a Reservation Agent. Evangelist then spoke to me saying, "God is going to promote you on your job because you obeyed Him." I really was not sure just what she meant and was pretty clueless. I kept what she said in the back of my mind, and I turned it over to God.

While I was in prayer one morning, the Holy Spirit spoke to me and said, "Ask what you will. You have not because you ask not." A year later, they hired a new manager for the department, and she took me under her wing and began to train me in every area of management. Someone said to me one day, "You need to stop letting them use you, and you are not getting anywhere with them." On the contrary, the Holy Spirit just kept on saying, "glean all you can" so I continued to learn as much as I could.

The next year, that manager left leaving no one to manage the department. At that point, I took it upon myself, and I picked up the slack. I used every bit of knowledge that I had learned, and it paid off. A few months later, I was offered the management position. Being the manager of the hotel was a wonderful opportunity. It was then that I saw the miracle hands of God move. I had a young lady by the name of Kim working as one of my reservation agents. She came into work one day and was crying, so I walked towards her to find out what was wrong. She explained to me that she had just came back from the doctor and they told her they had discovered a tumor in her uterus which might be cancerous (she was only twenty-one). She was crying so hard it was very difficult to understand to her. Having access to the rooms, I immediately told her to come with me to one of the rooms. When we got into the room, the first thing I asked her is if she believed that God could heal her. She responded by saying, "Yes," and that was all I needed. She turned to me and said, "But I am a Catholic." I responded by saying, "God doesn't care what you are, He just loves you."

My next question was, "Do you believe in prayer?" She said, "Yes," then I said, "Let's pray." I laid my hands on her and told her to believe, she responded that she did. The Holy Spirit spoke a word to her through me that when she would go back to the doctor, the tumor would no longer be there. I immediately responded by saying, "Be healed in Jesus' name."

She had an appointment set up for the next week because they were going to remove the tumor, so I told her to make sure they retest her before they do anything, and she did just that. When they retested her, they could not find the tumor. She said she screamed out, "God did it!" and they looked at her strangely.

"Deep in my heart I know God did it!" she exclaimed to me. She became a believer in prayer and in total healing.

This reminded me of Mark 3:1-5 when Jesus healed the man with the withered hand on the Sabbath day. The thought came to me that day as I prayed for Kim that this is not the place where you should be praying for someone because you are in the workplace. It was unprofessional, but I was not going to let the opportunity go by when someone needed a miracle. God doesn't care where you are if you are willing to be used by Him.

I continued to use different rooms in the hotel to minister to my employees as the opportunity arose. Many of their lives were changed through prayer and confessing the Word of God. During these times, I had several promotions and opportunities with the company. God continued to bless me year in and year out. It was unbelievable. I was reminded of II Samuel 7:29: *Therefore, now let it please Thee to bless the house of Thy servant, that it may continue forever before Thee: for Thou, O Lord God, hast spoken it: and with Thy blessing let the house of Thy servant be blessed forever.*

Evangelist Brinson continued to pour into me, while I continued with the prayer group. My niece attended the prayer service with me one morning. After about fifteen minutes of praying, she began to convulse, and foam filled her mouth. This was unfamiliar territory for me, so I did what I knew how to do, and that was to pray. The Evangelist took over and began to rebuke that spirit in her. I was frightened because I had never experienced anything like this before. She immediately sensed my fear, and she boldly said, "Don't be afraid but believe, and keep praying in the Spirit." I began to pray in the Spirit as hard as I could, then a few minutes later, I felt a strong boldness.

I began to take authority over that spirit, then the Evangelist instructed me to lay hands on my niece. I did as I was instructed. While praying with everything in me, for a minute I allowed my mind to drift, and that demonic spirit jumped off her straight into my throat and I started coughing. By comparison I remembered immediately what happened to Peter when he took his eyes off Jesus in Matthew 14:28-31. As soon as I realized what happened, I quickly refocused, took authority over that spirit, and immediately it left.

I laid my hand on my niece and commanded the spirit to leave, and it did. She fell to the ground soaking wet from sweat, repeatedly asking what had happened. She looked like a brand-new person, as if someone took a mask off her face. She kept repeating the words, "I am free, I am free, I am free." These scriptures were read so she could understand what was going on with her:

Matthew 8:16 - *When the evening was come, they brought unto Him many that were possessed with devils: and He cast out the spirits with His word, and healed all that were sick.*

Acts 8:7 - *For unclean spirits, crying with loud voice, came out of many that were possessed with them: and many taken with palsies and that were lame, were healed.*

Acts 16:16 - *And it came to pass, as we went to prayer, a certain damsel possessed with a spirit of divination met us, which brought her masters much gain by soothsaying.*

My niece turned to me and said, "Auntie Debbie, I want to stay in prayer with you all the time. Prayer does change things."

I would travel back and forth to different conferences with the International Prayer Connection every year since, and I witnessed many lives changed through prayer. There is no other explanation, this is the result of accepting the call to meet God at 5:00 a.m. in the mornings. Some people make excuses and would say that is too early, or I need my sleep, or that doesn't make any sense, but I am telling you that if you want to get acquainted with the Almighty, you will have to sacrifice something to get to your destiny. Prayer is one way of building a relationship with the Father, Son, and Holy Spirit. It is a time of fellowship with Him. It is the only way to be in unity with the Spirit and it's your time to receive wisdom, knowledge, and understanding of the Word of God. This is where revelation comes alive in you, and you are ready to slap a bear or two.

Through the Holy Spirit, I learned the ten steps of how to start my days with God which is a practice I continue to this day. Patterns have changed, words have changed, but I stayed consistent with these steps and they have been life-changing for me.

## 10 Steps to Start Your Day with God

### Step 1: Acknowledge God

*"Lord, I come before You today and thank You that You are my heavenly Father. You are El Shaddai, the Lord God Almighty. You are the Father which art in heaven and Holy is Thy name. You are Alpha and Omega, the beginning and the ending, which is, and which was, and which is to come. You are the great I Am, and I thank you."*

Use every name you can think of that applies to the King of Kings. What most of us don't know is that God desires for us to love Him like we would love our spouses or children. He wants to feel that same intimacy. These are moments when you just love on Him because He is God, and you are not looking for anything in return.

> *"Thank You for the air that I breathe. Thank You for waking me up today. Thank You for when I have and when I don't. Thank You for the good times and bad. Thank you for keeping watch over me and my children. Thank You for Your protection from danger, seen and unseen. Thank You for when I go out and when I come in. Thank You for life, health and strength. Thank You for supplying all my needs according to Your riches in glory by Christ Jesus. Thank You for my friends, my spiritual leaders, and everyone who surrounds me."*

Thank Him for everything. Below is just another example. You do not have to say the same things that I have written as it is only a guideline of how you should start your day with God. As you mature in the Lord, He will give you your own style but be consistent in everything that you do.

**Step 2: Praise God**

> *"Lord, I praise You for Who You are and all that You have done."*

We were created to worship because it brings us into the presence of God which in turn allows us to receive instruction.

*"Lord, I come not because of what You can do, but because I am indebted to You. You are to be exalted above all else. I come to You because I am grateful, and I want to show my gratitude, and as the scripture says, It is a good thing to give thanks unto the Lord."*

Show up with the spirit of expectancy and reverence. When I say expect, I mean to expect a sudden change to take place in you. Expect because He is the supernatural, and well abled God.

When you praise, everything you need for that moment is supplied immediately when you begin to reverence Him. Don't focus on material things but on those things, that are *above* such as winning souls for the Kingdom of God. Praise Him for lives being changed. Praise Him for drawing men and women to Him. Praise Him for destroying bondages. Praise Him for healing someone else other than yourself. Praise Him for bringing your children and loved ones back into the fold. Praise Him for the next generation of young adults coming back into true worship. When you do this, you are following the order according to the

Word in Matthew 6:33, *But seek ye first the kingdom of God, and His righteousness; and all these things shall be added unto you.*

Psalm 34:1-2 – *I will bless the LORD at all times: Your praise will continually be in my mouth. My soul boasts in You Lord; I'll forever humble myself while I hear from You.* Understand what the scripture is saying - bless Him when you are up or down. Bless Him when you just lost a loved one, or you got fired from your job. Don't just bless Him when you find yourself with other material blessings, because sometimes those blessings could be a distraction and not from Him anyway.

According *to* Proverbs 10:22 (ESV): *The blessing of the Lord makes rich, and He adds no sorrow with it.* So, think about that $50,000 car you are stressing over and ask yourself this question: "Is this really a blessing?" For if it is, I should be stress-free. This type of praise will keep you from making errors or making the wrong choices; it will keep you in tuned with the voice of God.

**Step 3: Choose one of God's names, attributes or characteristics and thank Him for being that to you**

**El Shaddai:** *God Almighty, The Mighty One of Jacob* - Genesis 49:24 – speaks of God's ultimate power over all.

*"You are stronger and more powerful than anything I face or any enemy that opposes me."*

**Elohim:** *God, Creator, Mighty and Strong* (Genesis 17:7; Jeremiah 31:33) – the plural form of *Eloah*, which accommodates the doctrine of the Trinity.[23] From the Bible's first sentence, the superlative nature of God's power is evident as God (Elohim) speaks the world into existence (Genesis 1:1).

> *"You are my deliverer, counselor, my peace, my reward, my shield and buckler, my refiner, my overcomer. You are the God who forgives, the God who loves, the God who gives peace. I praise You for all this and then some. You are my healer, my comforter, my redeemer, my forgiver, my strength, my resting place, my provider, my light, and my refuge from the storm, and I thank You for being that."*

**Adonai:** *Lord* (Genesis 15:2; Judges 6:15) – used in place of YHWH, which was thought by the Jews to be too sacred to be uttered by sinful men. In the Old Testament, YHWH is more often used in God's dealings with His people, while *Adonai* is used more when He deals with the Gentiles.

**Jehovah-Jireh:** *The Lord Will Provide* (Genesis 22:14) – the name memorialized by Abraham when God provided the ram to be sacrificed in place of Isaac.

**Jehovah Shalom:** *The Lord Our Peace* (Judges 6:24) – the name given by Gideon to the altar he built after the Angel of the Lord assured him he would not die as he thought he would after seeing Him. We need the peace of God that passes all understanding during our time of prayer and devotion. A peace that transcends beyond our own imagination because this solemn time is when the enemy tries to bombard your mind with everything other than prayer. Keep in mind there are many more names of God that can be used and these are just a few.

**Step 4: Present Your Day**

*"Lord, I present my day to You, and I ask you to bless it in every way. Lord, You oversee my day and put it in order, so I have far fewer unpleasant surprises. I am setting my day before You and putting it in Your hands. I surrender my all to You, my worries, anxiety, loneliness, sadness, depression, despair, and pain. I surrender my day to You. In all my ways I acknowledge You, and You shall direct thy paths. I fear You LORD, and I depart from evil. And it shall*

be health to my navel, and marrow to my bones. Lord, I lift before You my job and my church, the plans I must develop, the things I need to do, the decisions I have to make, the talks I need to have, the bills I have to pay, the letters I have to write and all that's ahead of me."

Lay it all on the altar and rid yourself of world systems that are keeping you from connecting to the Spirit of God. This is the moment that you want to know that the Almighty is hearing you.

**Step 5: Present Your Body**

"Lord, I present my body to You this day as a living sacrifice, and I ask You to help me be a good steward of this temple of Your Spirit. Romans 12:1 says my body is a living sacrifice, holy and acceptable to You. I submit my entire being totally to You, and I acknowledge my dependence upon You physically, spiritually and emotionally."

According to 1 Corinthians 6:17,19-20, You said, "He that is joined unto the Lord is one spirit and that my body is the temple of the Holy Ghost which is in me, which I have of God. I am not my own for I am bought with a price, *therefore, I must glorify God in my body, and in my spirit, which are God's"*.

All Christians should submit daily to God as part of their walk with Him. This is a part of taking up one's cross daily (Luke 9:23). However, the intent of Romans 12:1 is *not* such a daily submission. It is a once-and-for-all-time dedication, surrender, and submission to Him. It is the sacrifice of one's life unconditionally and permanently to God as a living, holy, and acceptable sacrifice. It is a voluntary life-long commitment back to Him for His glory and for His unrestricted use. In *Romans 12:1*, the believer is both priest and sacrifice. As part of the great mercies accomplished by Jesus as priest and sacrifice of our salvation, we are exhorted to present our bodies as sacrifices to God.

Salvation was accomplished by the sacrificial death of Jesus. Each believer needs to make a second decision beyond salvation to dedicate himself or herself to God, once and for all submitting to Him. There is a good example of this kind of voluntary and permanent commitment in Deuteronomy 15:12-17. Freed Hebrew slaves could choose to re-sell themselves to their masters. That choice was based on the past mercies of the slave master, which was prompted by the slave's love for the master. If the slave master agreed to reaccept the slave, this decision was permanent. Then an awl was used to pierce the slave's ear, signifying that he was the master's servant *forever*. That is the same type of rededication or recommitment as the Romans 12:1 sacrifice. This re-enlistment is not forced slavery instead it is the freed slave's choice. It is his once-and-for-all-time decision.

**Step 6: Confess - Proper Confession**
1 John 1:8-9 – God Your Word says,
> *"If we say that we have no sin, we deceive ourselves, and the truth is not in us." You must also say, "If I confess my sins, You are faithful and just to forgive me of all my sins and cleanse me from all unrighteousness."*

Before confession, attempt to recall all sins committed, both voluntarily or involuntarily. Then re-examine your life to recall not only those sins committed since the last confession but also those which have not been confessed through forgetfulness. Then, with compunction and a contrite heart, approach the cross and begin the confession of your sins.

1. We should confess our sins honestly, remembering that we open them not to a man, but to God Himself. God knows our sins already and only wants our admission of them. We should not be embarrassed before God because once He has forgiven us, they

are under the Blood. He took the burden of sin, so He could identify with us. He is aware of our human shortcomings as well as man's tendency towards sin. For this reason, our spiritual Father cannot be our terrible judge at confession.

Let me ask a question. Sometimes don't we become embarrassed of our sin and think that our spiritual Father would have a lessor opinion of us? On the contrary, He will have even more love for us when He sees that we are open and honest in our confession. Furthermore, if we are afraid to reveal our sins before Him, how will we overcome our shame and regret when you appear at His Last Judgment? There, all our sins which we have not confessed will be opened before Him, the angels and all people.

2. We need to be specific when we confess, listing all our sins separately. We must not only say: "I have sinned, or I am sinful," but we must declare each type of sin. *"The Revelation of Sins,"* says St. Basil the Great, "is subject to the same law as the Declaration of Physical ills."[24] The sinner is spiritually ill, and the spiritual Father is the physician or healer. It stands to reason that we must confess or tell about our sins in the same way as when we are physically ill, describe the symptoms of our illness to a doctor from whom we expect to receive healing.

## Step 7: Speak Words that bring Life

*"Lord, may the words of my mouth and the meditation of my heart always be acceptable in Your sight. May they bring life and truth to everyone who hears them. Lord, Your Word says that the preparations of the heart belong to man, but the answer of the tongue is from the Lord". It also says that "out of the abundance of the heart the mouth speaks. Prepare my heart by filling it with Your Word. Please monitor my mouth so that every word that proceeds from my lips is loving, truthful, kind, comforting, edifying, wise, encouraging, and God-glorifying."*


## Death and Life are in the Power of the Tongue

As part of our sanctification process with the Lord, we need to expect Him to target three principal areas in our walk with Him. The first area will be with our *thought life* – which is the area of our unspoken words. In this sanctification process, one of the first things we will find that the Lord will want to do is to try and put right thinking into our minds and thought processes. The people who always seem to be more happy, upbeat, and fulfilled with their lives are the people who have a good sound mind and who are always thinking about or dwelling on the more positive things in this life. They choose of their own free will to dwell on the more positive side of this life versus always thinking and dwelling on the darker and negative side. The people who are not happy and fulfilled and who are always pessimistic and depressed and have negative attitudes towards anybody and anything. They are choosing to think and dwell on the negative side of this life. The power lies with us. We cannot blame anyone else, including God, if we have chosen with our own free will to constantly dwell on the negativity.

The second area God will be targeting will be our *word life* – which must do with the words that are being released out of our mouths. Our *word life* with others will make or break us in your own personal relationships. If we do not learn how to speak to other people in a positive and godly manner, then sooner or later, no one will want to have anything to do with us, and we will eventually find ourselves being totally isolated and alone. As children of God, we should all work very closely with the Holy Spirit in allowing Him to help us clean up our word life and express ourselves to other people. If we can learn how to get this part of our lives properly cleaned up and sanctified under His direction and guidance, then not only will we become more pleasing to the Lord, but we will also dramatically increase the quality of our own personal relationships.

*But shun profane and idle babblings, for they will increase to more ungodliness. And their message will spread like cancer* (2 Timothy 2:16-17, NKJV).

The third area God will be targeting will be our *action life* – which is how we act and behave towards others. Our actions and behavior toward others should always line up with our sanctified thinking and our sanctified speech. The Bible says we must be *doers* of the Word, and not just hearers.

1. *In all labor there is profit, but idle chatter leads only to poverty* (Proverbs 14:23, NKJV)
2. *A talebearer reveals secrets, but he who is of a faithful spirit conceals a matter* (Proverbs 11:13, NKJV)
3. *A brother offended is harder to win than a strong city* (Proverbs 18:19, NKJV)
4. *A perverse man sow's strife and a whisperer separates the best of friends* (Proverbs 16:28, NKJV)
5. *But he who repeats a matter separates friends* (Proverbs 17:9, NKJV)

**Step 8: Ask for What You Need**
*"Lord, I ask You to meet all of my needs today. Specifically, I ask for the following things..."* then we may petition the Lord for all our needs. Ask according to scriptures, which

is the will of God. James 4:2 - *Ye have not because ye ask not.* (Note: This verse in context does teach us to ask according to His will and not your desires, but the point remains).

Philippians 4:6 - *Be careful about nothing; but in everything by prayer and supplication with thanksgiving let your requests be made known unto God.* The most powerful prayer of petition is a written petition. Why do I believe this? Because it becomes more specific when you take the time to write it out. When Jesus was asked by his followers how to pray, He gave us what is known today as the Lord's Prayer. So many people pray that prayer every day exactly as He gave it to us, not realizing that praying that scripture verbatim is really missing the point. He was not telling us what to pray but how to pray.

Matthew 6:9 - *After this manner, therefore, pray ye:* He said, "*after this manner*," He didn't say, "Pray this." In other words, pray like this. He didn't say, "This is what I want you to say when you pray." In fact, a couple of verses before that, He condemned using vain repetitions. So, isn't it weird that right after He told us not to use repetitions to the point of calling it vain He would then immediately give us a prayer to repeat? It's not weird at all because He wasn't giving us a prayer to repeat, He was giving us an example of how to pray. I brought this up because part of that prayer was an example of the prayer of petition, the prayer of asking for things we need.

## Step 9: Pray for God's Will in Your Life

Matthew 6:10 - *Your will be done.*

> *"Lord, may Your will be done in my life this day and every day till Your Kingdom comes, Your will be done, on earth as it is in heaven.*

This is a very difficult part of Jesus' prayer. It is so often overlooked. We are to pray according to God's will. We are to pray what God's desire, what God decides, what God wants, and what God commands. You see, prayer is not just asking Him for things we want even though that is included but we should begin with an attitude of respect and praise, and then seek His will.

John states that if we have confidence in approaching God, then we know that something will happen when we pray. We can be confident that our prayers are effective and powerful! God answers our prayers according to His will, which is what is truly best for our own wellbeing. We all hit periods in life where it seems that God just isn't listening to our prayers. It seems like we pray, and nothing is happening. During those times we need to grab hold of Romans 8:28 (NIV) and not let go. He promises that, *we know that in all things [even the bad things] God works for the good of those who love Him, who have been called according to His purpose.* We can then have confidence that even when it seems like God isn't listening, He is.

Matthew 6:11 - *Give us this day our daily bread.* Look at how specific He told us to pray for things we need. What do we want? We want Him to give us something. What is that? Bread. When do we want it? This day. What does bread represent? It represents the Word - the bread of life. This is very specific and detailed how He wants us to ask Him for things.

At times we might say that we don't need to prove to God what was asked for because He will remember, but will we? Writing things down on paper is a very powerful way to communicate anything. There can be no misunderstanding when something is written down. Just like a contract. Sure, an oral contract is just as binding as a written one, but try proving in a court of law exactly what was said and how it was said. A written contract leaves out all doubt as to what was promised and expected of each person involved because it is specific and recorded. We are the ones who should have faith that we will receive what we asked for. We are the ones who needs to remember our requests to Him.

## Step 10: Pray for other People

*"Lord, I pray for the following people..."* Then list all who come to mind or pray from a prayer list that was previously prepared. Start with the people closest like immediate family members and close friends. Mention each one by name and bring them under the covering of God's blessings. Next pray for our church, the people we will likely see in our day. We then need to ask God to show us whom we should be praying for during the day. He may suggest someone we don't even know so that we can adopt them in prayer. Remember the logical extension of our devotional time with the Lord is intercessory prayer. We will naturally turn to prayer for others when we've been alone with God.

Communication with our heavenly Father is more than a cozy, open invitation to come to Him anytime, anywhere. Even though His ears are open to the cries of His children twenty-four-seven. Prayer is much more than that. It is also an act of obedience. We are exhorted to pray for others and to pray without ceasing. Another even more amazing mystery is that when we pray for someone else, we change. All of us were made to be loved, to give and to receive love. When our hearts connect through prayer to the One who is the source of true love, we'll find that praying for others will wondrously result in our hearts being changed – when this happens, our lives will be transformed.

After completion of the ten steps with God, obey, believe, and receive, knowing that whatever we ask is already done. *He is not a man that would lie* (Numbers 23:19).

# Chapter 9

## Intimacy with God

The definition of intimacy is:

1. A close, familiar, and usually affectionate or loving personal relationship with another person or group.

2. A close association with or detailed knowledge or deep understanding of a place, subject, period of history, etc.

3. An intimate quality or state: such as emotional warmth and closeness.

Intimacy generally refers to the feeling of being in a close personal association and belonging together. It is a familiar and very close affective connection with another because of a bond that is formed through knowledge and experience of the other. Genuine intimacy in human relationships requires dialogue, transparency, vulnerability, and reciprocity. According to Webster's Dictionary, reciprocity means a reciprocal condition or relationship, a mutual or cooperative interchange of favors or privileges, especially information.

We are called to dwell in the secret place of the Most High! To gaze upon His beauty, to hear the cry of His heart and linger in His presence. In that place of intimacy is where we can dwell. Psalm 91:1 (AMP) - *He who dwells in the secret place of the Most High shall remain stable and fixed under the shadow of the Almighty [Whose power no foe can withstand].*

Other definitions to keywords are:

**Dwell**
To make one's home to reside, to live or linger over in thought or speech: to think about or discuss at length.

**Secret**
1. Kept from public knowledge or from the knowledge of a certain person or persons.
2. Withdrawn, remote or secluded, hideaway.
3. Keeping one's affairs to oneself, beyond general knowledge or understanding, somewhat mysterious.

4. Concealed from sight or hidden, something not revealed understood or explained.

**Abide**
1. To stand fast; remain or go on being

2. To stay or reside, in or at, to await; to submit to or put up with.

3. To live up to (agreement) to submit to and carry out (rule).

God wants us to spend time with Him and intimately communicate with Him enjoying fellowship, trusting and following His lead. This is what gives our lives meaning and purpose. Our souls are being called into obedience through our spirit, by the wooing of the Holy Spirit! The carnality of man is being called into glory!

The soul of man longs for fulfillment. Many people, even in the church, try to fill this longing with activities, meetings, seminars, and works. The truth is, our soul will not be satisfied until it has come into intimacy with the Living God!

Our re-born spirit already knows that God is calling us into intimacy - body, soul, and spirit! It is the secret place of God where He re-positions our hearts. When the human heart is connected to the Spirit of God, the two become as one knitted together and the joy of being in His presence bubbles over. It is a joy to Jesus when a person takes the time to walk more intimately with Him. God sees us as a precious treasure, and He longs to have a close relationship with us. More than anything, His desire is to have an intimate, love relationship and friendship.

Eyes, ears, and our minds can't contain all that is God! It is like trying to measure the volume of the Pacific Ocean with a teacup. In the natural, our senses (taste, touch, sight, hearing, smell) cannot comprehend God and His fullness; and yet in the spirit, we are given eyes to see the invisible, ears to hear the inaudible, and minds that conceive the inconceivable.

The Hebrew word "yada" which is used in the Old Testament means *to know Him*.[25] It is translated into English as the word "know" or "knowledge," but the Hebrew word has a much wider sweep and meaning than the English translation. In the Old Testament, this word for knowing God means the following: to perceive, to learn, to understand, to recognize, to believe, to accept His claims, to conform, to be willing, to perform, to live, to obey, to see or experience. We should "yada" and hold important the keys to getting to know God the way that He wants us to know Him. The opposite of knowing God is not ignorance or a lack of knowledge but is rebellion.

Intimacy with God is the fullest possible fellowship and partnership with Him comes as we desire and seek to know Him,

His plans, His will and His ways. Prayer and spending time with Him is all about our desire and passion for Him. It is not a "religious" discipline in our Christian walk. Religiosity has taken over the church, so much so that people can't even recognize when the Spirit of God is present. Religion can be very different than having a relationship with God through Jesus Christ. Religions are man-made and are based on trying to get to God through rules, regulations and works.

We should not allow our quiet time to become a religious expression. It should be a time of bringing our soul into submission to the Spirit. If we continue to do this, then our growth will be a religious growth and not a spiritual one. God's way to reach man is through Jesus, but man's way is through religion. The more we know about God, the more we will love Him and of course, the more intimate we will become with Him. What a most tender friendship Enoch had with God during their contracted time - their intimate communion lasting for over three hundred years! If we would like to enjoy the same blessedness, then we must, like Enoch, walk with God. Genesis 5:24 - *And Enoch walked with God: and he was not; for God took him.*

Enoch was the father of Methuselah (longest living person in the Bible), and the great-grandfather of Noah. It is said of him that he walked with God after the birth of Methuselah for three hundred years. It was a long time for a man to support a holy life and communion with God without any relapse worthy of notice. It is difficult for Christians now to do this for a single day. How remarkable then that he should have done it for that longevity! Such approval did his extraordinary piety gain him that when the time came for him to leave the earth, God "translated" him (like He did to Elijah) and suffered him not to taste the bitterness of death. Perhaps this was to show mankind what He would have done for them had they never sinned.

Can you imagine what it would feel like if we knew no sin and walked this closely with God? Just picture if our parents understood our purpose and groomed us in the way that God intended where we could have been intimate with Him. We would have been living in His presence daily without reservation and hesitation. Our lives would be so fulfilled that it would be easy for us to obey His every command. With this in mind, let's teach our children their purpose so they can live that fulfilled life in God.

John 15:4 - *Abide in Me, and I in you. As the branch cannot bear fruit of itself, except it abides in the vine; no more can ye, except ye abide in Me.*

True intimacy requires two things: to be in consistent fellowship with someone and to be loyal to that person. In John 15, Jesus instructs us about the essential dynamic of abiding with Him. He is the vine, and we are the branches. We all know that a branch is unable to survive if it is separated from the vine.

People in intimate relationships, often called a couple, especially if the members of that couple have ascribed some degree of permanency to their relationship. Such couples often provide the emotional security that is necessary for them to accomplish other tasks, particularly forms of labor or work. When we become one with God, He teaches us what true relationship is all about.

We can also learn from the Word of God how to develop genuine relationships in the natural. The way we give our entire time and feeling to man is what God desires from us. He wants us to be secure in Him completely and allow Him to be the *husbandman* to us as He said in His Word. Let's define *husbandman* and see what Jesus was really saying:

> husbandman - a person who operates a farm
> - farmer, granger, sodbuster

Jesus described the Father as the Creator of all the things so, from the beginning of time, God's intention for us was to grow continually in Him, stay connected to the vine, and be fruitful and multiply - not in having babies but in winning souls for the Kingdom. When you think about it, God went down deep into the gutter to bring us out. Intimacy with God gives you the true revelation of being connected to the vine. We are to produce crops

- witnessing to the lost and the hurting - not just talking about it, but doing something about it. That is what true intimacy teaches.

Abide means "to live in." This is the goal where we can live up to that expectation of living in God and Him living in us. If we could focus our thoughts on Him, then we could do all things through Him and only do things which He approves. Keeping the mind focused is very hard at times because our flesh gets distracted by worldly things which then takes precedence in our minds. We should not allow that to happen. One way of avoiding that pitfall is to dive into the Word with much prayer and fasting, because the more we commune with Him, the closer we will grow in Him. His omnipresence enables Him to also dwells in the believer. The indwelling of His is given to all who believe.

1 Corinthians 3:16 (ESV) - *Do you not know that you are God's temple and that God's Spirit dwells in you?* However, His omnipresence and the indwelling of His Spirit does not stop us from longing after the presence of God. How can we long and hunger for something that is already all around us and dwells within us? When we talk about experiencing the presence of the Lord, we are really talking about the realization of abiding in His presence.

He speaks to us through His Word, throughout the scriptures. He also speaks to us in our hearts and minds. We become more familiar with His will through what we read in the Word. Discovering the Word of God is like discovering hidden treasures. *Matthew 13:44 (NLT) - The Kingdom of Heaven is like a treasure that a man discovered hidden in a field. In his excitement, he hid it again and sold everything he owned to get enough money to buy the field.* This parable is intended to instruct believers to prefer the Kingdom of Heaven and not the world, denying themselves and all the desires of the flesh so that nothing may prevent them from obtaining the treasures God has for them.

**Strengthening Your Relationship with God**

1. Talk to God daily in a normal, everyday type of conversation. Remember that God can read our minds and that He is constantly observing our innermost thoughts, so He is quite aware of what is going on in our hearts and minds - far better than we even do. So, our conversations with God can be vocal, or we can silently talk to Him through our thoughts anytime we desire. He gave us a little taste of His ability to search the hearts of men and read their minds back in Jeremiah 17:10 (NASB) when He said, *"I, the Lord, search the heart, I test the mind, even to give to each man according to his ways, According to the results of his deeds."* So, we can easily talk to God in our thoughts, and these conversations can be done anytime or anyplace.

2. The second thing we need to do in order to better communicate with God is to read His Word every day. Only by reading the very Word of God can we hope to draw near to Him. I can't stress enough that prayer and the Word are the keys to ultimate ecstasy in God. Before I understood the Word, I thought God would answer me in some divine way or somehow speak to me verbally out of the heavens, but that isn't the way God operates. God speaks to a person's heart and their mind.

I used to ask the question, "Why bother to listen to God because God always seems to work in such mysterious ways?" I would say that I had absolutely no idea how or why God does what He does, however, with knowledge and understanding as a true believer, God's ways are not mysterious. His ways are not concealed behind smoke and mirrors. It is just the opposite, because once we begin to understand Jesus Christ, once we begin to learn what He is all about, once we begin to understand what He is trying to do in this world and in our lives, once we begin to understand the tremendous importance that He holds for all of mankind, then His actions will not be mysterious. In fact, that's when His ways become crystal clear. For that is when the veil over our eyes is lifted.

James 4:8 - *Draw nigh to God, and He will draw nigh to you.* This must be clearly understood considering the perfection of God's immensity and omnipresence. We draw nigh to God when we *present our bodies as a living sacrifice, holy and acceptable unto Him.* When we tread in his courts and attend to His ordinances, there we will always find how beneficial it is for us to draw nigh unto Him.

Roberta Flack and Donny Hathaway sang this song together back in 1978, "The closer I get to you; the more you'll make me see, by giving you all I've got, your love has captured me..."[26] This is what we should be feeling towards our Heavenly Father when we draw nigh to Him. This song should have been written to God and not to man. We should be so captivated by His presence that not even the very breath we breathe can be heard.

Remember the prodigal son in Luke 15:11-32? When the son returned home, his dad ran to meet him. That is what God is waiting to do when we make up in our minds to get closer to Him.

Although God is always with us, it is obvious that there are times when His presence is with us in greater measure, and we experience His intimate presence in a greater capacity. The manifest presence of God is what brings power. God's manifest presence is what changes lives and reveals the glory of God. God reveals Himself to those who earnestly seek Him (Deuteronomy

4:29). If we want to walk in the presence of the Lord, then we need to be practicing the presence of God. One of the major ways we can do this is through worship. By placing ourselves before Him in a place of adoration, we make room for Him. Through focusing our attention on Him, we increase our awareness of being in His presence. Learning how to soak in God's presence through worship is one of the most valuable things we can do with our time.

Worship is also a form of praying. It is the position and place where we no longer focus on self but give God all the glory that's due to Him. It is a place of instruction and revelation from the heart of God. This is one of my favorite scriptures that I repeat when I feel my flesh trying to overtake my spirit: Ephesians 5:17-20 - *Wherefore be ye not unwise, but understanding what the will of the Lord is. And be not drunk with wine, wherein is excess; but be filled with the Spirit; speaking to yourselves in psalms and hymns and spiritual songs, singing and making melody in your heart to the Lord; giving thanks always for all things unto God and the Father in the name of our Lord Jesus Christ.*

During these intimate moments, God would give me songs. Here is one which was inspired by Psalms 91.

> *Sing unto the Lord a new song, sing unto the Lord all the earth, sing unto the Lord, bless His name; sing*

*unto the Lord all the earth. Worship Him, worship Him, and sing unto the Lord all the earth.*

Paul says in Philippians 3:10 (AMP) - *[For my determined purpose is] that I may know Him [that I may progressively become more deeply and intimately acquainted with Him, perceiving and recognizing and understanding the wonders of His Person more strongly and more clearly], and that I may in that same way come to know the power outflowing from His resurrection [which it exerts over believers], and that I may so share His sufferings as to be continually transformed [in spirit into His likeness even] to His death, [in the hope].* In this verse, we find the apostle's goal for life. Paul refers to it as his "determined purpose." Nothing can be more important for a child of God. Deep things are intriguing, and there is nothing like depth to make us dissatisfied with superficial and shallow things. God's desire is for us to go deeper rather than being content to remain on the surface of things.

In April 2005, I was in prayer before the Lord with one of my prayer partners (who has since gone on to be with the Lord). It was an intense, intimate moment with the Lord that night. I remember that night he called and said, "Let's pray." On the phone, we shared some testimonies and some scriptures, and then we began to pray. I started out by worshiping the Lord, and then I got so lost in the presence of God that I forgot I was on the phone.

I entered a place of pure ecstasy where I could see myself floating. I was out of my own body, and the more I worshiped, the more I felt the presence of God in the room. There was a song that I could hear in the heavens that was very soothing. I could hear every instrument playing in harmony. I then looked straight in front of me, and I could see a cloud forming. As it began to take shape, I saw this person dressed as a bride, adorned in white and a veil which covered her face.

The sight was so mesmerizing that I could not look away. Then I saw the form of a man with bright lights around Him, and he was also in white. The bride was walking towards this man, and she was moving slowly, but directly towards Him. His hands were extended out towards her as she approached. The closer the person got, the more I wanted to see who was under that veil.

I kept my eyes fixed on that lady, and as she reached close to Him, she stopped, and His hands were still extended out to her. He raised the veil, and when I looked, it was me! And still, in awe of the Spirit, I said, "It is me!" Tears began to run down my face. The voice then spoke to me and said, *"You are the bride of Christ,"* and then He smiled and began to drift. I remember asking the question, "Lord is it You? Lord, is it You? Lord, is it You?" He looked up at me and said, *"Yes, it is."* At that moment, He let my hands go and walked away. To this day, I don't know why He appeared to me in that form, but all I know is that it was the most intimate moment I have ever had, and it is one that cannot be explained.

I realized there was a silence on the phone and the person on the other end was not praying at all. It took at least thirty minutes of silence before I could speak. I remember him saying to me, "Sister Debbie, what happened? Something happened while we were praying - something happened!" I responded and said, "I can't explain what happened, but all I know is I had an encounter with God." He replied, "I know because I could hear you. The heavens opened up!"

When entering a place like this, it is unexplainable in the natural sense. Sometimes there are no words to describe what the experience that you have encountered except that you know without a shadow of a doubt that you were in the presence of God. Once these types of moments have passed, you can't bring them back like you would go back to read a scripture or study a book, so lock these intimate times in your heart and never let them go.

When we begin to learn how to worship God in the Spirit, it causes changes to take place in us. According to John 4:24 - *God is a Spirit and they that worship Him must worship Him in spirit and in truth.* When the Spirit of Truth is present and revealed, change takes place.

# Chapter 10

# Praying with a Broken Heart

The definition of *broken* is:

1. violently separated into parts: shattered
2. damaged or altered by breaking: as

   a: having undergone or been subjected to fracture.

   b: being irregular, interrupted, or full of obstacles

   c: violated by transgression.

   d: discontinuous interruption

   e: disrupted by change.

   f: having an irregular, streaked, or blotched pattern especially from virus infection

3. made weak or infirmed

   a: subdued completely: crushed, sorrowful (a *broken* heart) (a *broken* spirit) b: bankrupt

       c: reduced in rank

4. cut off: disconnected

       a: imperfectly spoken or written

       b: not complete or full

5. disunited by divorce, separation, or desertion.

When I found out my ex-husband was cheating on me, my heart was violently shattered into pieces, and my emotions were damaged. It was one of the hardest things I ever had to go through. The question is, did I stop praying because I found myself in this dilemma? Did I stop serving God because this situation was upon me? Well, the answer is "No!" I did not stop praying - I could not stop praying.

The situation allowed me to seek God even more because I realized I was inadequate without Him. I remembered it was the same God who spoke to me about meeting Him at 5:00 a.m. in the mornings for prayer. How could this God allow such a thing to happen to me? Well, He did not 'allow' my husband to cheat because my husband had a will to do or not to do. Could God have stopped him from doing this? Yes, but why would He go against His own Word?

Matthew 26:39 - 42 - *And He went a little farther, and fell on His face, and prayed, saying, O my Father, if it be possible, let this cup pass from Me: nevertheless, not as I will, but as thou will. He went away again the second time, and prayed, saying, O My Father, if this cup may not pass away from me, except I drink it, thy will be done.*

Jesus had the same opportunity as you and I have today. There is no difference. It's the same test and the same God. Why would God allow His only Son to suffer such a thing? Because He would not go against His Word. Matthew 24:35 - *Heaven and earth shall pass away, but my words shall not pass away.*

It was through prayer that I found out my husband was having an affair. The Holy Spirit showed me the whole picture, almost like I was watching a movie which would not end. During my time of early morning prayer, after my husband left for choir practice, the Holy Spirit instructed me to go on the computer. At first, I hesitated, but the voice kept on getting stronger in me. I even told myself it was the devil, but because I knew His voice and it was distinct, I could not shake it. I was computer illiterate at the time and did not even know how to even open up an email much less hack into someone else's mail. I decided to go back on my knees and pray just a little longer to make sure I was hearing right, and the same voice said, "I did not tell you to pray, but I instructed you to go on the computer. Believe you me?" I immediately obeyed! Obedience is better than sacrifice!

The Holy Spirit instructed me how to get on the computer and how to break into the codes, and He revealed everything to me! It was shocking and devastating, but it was at that time I understood the Word of God when it says in *Amos 3:7- Surely the Lord GOD will do nothing, but He reveals His secret unto His servants the prophets.* Truly my heart was broken into many pieces, but that's when God pressed me to pray even more. It was also during this time that people needed me the most and I had to go before the throne of grace on their behalf.

I was determined to stay in prayer fervently. One day the spirit of the Lord whispered. "Are you going to tuck your tail and regress back to your old ways or are you going to walk by faith, knowing that I can do exceedingly and abundantly more than you can even ask or think?"

The trust factor came into play. It was whether I could trust in the Lord with all my heart and lean not on my own understanding. There is one thing I have learned over the years and it is that, without faith it is impossible to please God. Faith without trust and belief is no faith at all and if that does not work, you can bet a million dollars that you won't be able to pray with a broken heart.

*Hebrews 11:1- Now faith is the substance of things hoped for, the evidence of things not seen.* Notice that hope is not birthed until faith is extended. What do I mean by that? What does faith have to do with praying? Well if my heart is broken, I must first exercise faith to hope that I can get a prayer through. Hope cannot come until you have faith. When we pray with a broken heart, we are hoping that God can mend our broken heart while we converse with Him. It is not guaranteed that our heart will be mended, or God will even answer us, it is simply faith being exercised which causes hope to come alive.

If you feel hopeless, step out in faith! Hopelessness comes from being broken or disappointed. Faith produces hope. If I am going to need faith to pray, I must find out the DNA of faith. If faith is a substance, then it is something tangible and something I can hold onto. I must lay faith out on the table and to find out where faith is pulled from. I must check its DNA and see who the father is. According to the scriptures, the father of faith is Abraham. We need to know what kind of father Abraham was. He is also the father of heartbreaks, disappointment, and sorrow - but that never stopped him from obeying the commands of God.

*Genesis 22:1-16 - And it came to pass after these things, that God did tempt Abraham, and said unto him, Abraham: and he said, Behold, here I am. And He said, take now thy son, thine only son Isaac, whom thou lovest, and get thee into the land of Moriah; and offer him there for a burnt offering upon one of the mountains which I will tell thee of. And Abraham rose early in the morning, and saddled his ass, and took two of his young men with him, and Isaac his son, and clave the wood for the burnt offering, and rose and went unto the place of which God had told him. Then on the third day, Abraham lifted his eyes and saw the place afar off. And Abraham said unto his young men, abide ye here with the ass; and I and the lad will go yonder and worship, and come again to you. And Abraham took the wood of the burnt offering, and laid it upon Isaac, his son; and he took the fire in his hand, and a knife; and they went both together. And Isaac spake unto Abraham, his father, and said, my father: and he said, here am I, my son. And he said, Behold the fire and the wood: but where is the lamb for a burnt offering?*

*And Abraham said, my son, God will provide himself a lamb for a burnt offering: so, they went together. And they came to the place which God had told him of; and Abraham built an altar there, and laid the wood in order, and bound Isaac, his son, and laid him on the altar upon the wood. And Abraham stretched forth his hand and took the knife to slay his son. And the angel of the LORD called unto him out of heaven, and said, Abraham, Abraham: and he said, here am I. And He said, lay not thine hand upon the lad, neither do thou anything unto him: for now, I know that thou fearest God, seeing thou hast not withheld thy son, thine only son from Me. And Abraham lifted his eyes, and looked, and behold behind him a ram caught in a thicket by his horns: and Abraham went and took the ram, and offered him up for a burnt offering instead of his son. And Abraham called the name of that place Jehovah Jireh: as it is said to this day, In the mount of the LORD it shall be seen. And the angel of the LORD called unto Abraham out of heaven the second time, and said, by myself have I sworn, saith the LORD, for because thou hast done this thing, and hast not withheld thy son, thine only son.*

Verse one says God tempted Abraham, but "tempt" used here means to put to the test, to try or to prove. This was not Abraham's first test. Between chapters 14-22 Abraham lived through a famine and still tithed. He said goodbye to his family and his father's home. He went to war to save a family member (Lot), who had turned his back on him. He interceded for a city that God already predetermined that He would destroy (Sodom). He buried his Lot's wife because she could not let go of the past. He was promised a child, feeling helpless that he couldn't see it happen. His wife told him to sleep with her servant Hagar. He slept with someone he did not love, nor did he even want to be with her, regardless, eventually produced a child who's named Ishmael. Abraham went through testing, trials, a broken heart, disappointment, and longsuffering.

When everything is falling apart around you, that is not the time to throw in the towel. Look at how faith manifested itself in Abraham as he stood in the face of adversity and looked at his child Isaac when God told him to sacrifice him, and said in his heart, "I will obey." He rose early the next day and got Isaac out of the bed and said, "Let's go." He got the wood, rope, knife, and fire. He was getting ready to go to the mountain to sacrifice his son. There was a struggle going on in the natural and the spiritual with Abraham. Then God said to Abraham, *"I want you to go to Mariah."* The word Mariah means Jehovah God has chosen. Notice the place where God has chosen. If you let God do the choosing, you will get the best He has for you.

When they got to the place where the sacrifice would take place, Abraham looked at the two men that were with him and told them, "You can't go any further with me." When you are getting ready to walk the miraculous, you must let go of the baggage because you cannot take everyone or everything with you - not even the donkey they rode on could go any further!

Now, why would God allow them to leave the very thing that is more stable? There are times you will have to climb your mountain and leave what you rode on to continue climbing and growing in Him. The thing that carried you to the place of sacrifice may not be the thing that can carry you to the place where

God wants you to be. You must get off what you are comfortable with and walk it by faith, even though your heart is overwhelmed. Isaiah 43:2 (NIV) - *When you pass through the waters, I will be with you; and when you pass through the rivers, they will not sweep over you. When you walk through the fire, you will not be burned; the flames will not set you ablaze.*

If you feel as though you are going through hell, go through it. The scripture teaches in Psalm 23:4 - *Yea, though I walk through the valley of the shadow of death I will fear no evil: for Thou art with me; Thy rod and Thy staff they comfort me.* You must go through hell because you don't want to stop there, the quicker you go through it, the greater the reward. Jesus went down to hell, and we all know what was His reward - Acts 2:31-33 - *He is seeing this before spoke of the resurrection of Christ, that his soul was not left in hell, neither his flesh did see corruption. This Jesus hath God raised up, whereof we all are witnesses. Therefore, being by the right hand of God exalted, and having received of the Father the promise of the Holy Ghost, He hath shed forth this, which ye now see and hear.*

God was about to give Abraham insight of what was going to take place four thousand years later, so he did not have time to stagger at God's promise or focus on the pain and sorrow because he was about to see the Kingdom of God unveiling itself. When Isaac realized that there was nothing to sacrifice, he questioned his father and Abraham answered, "The Lord will provide."

Abraham took the wood and placed it on the back of Isaac. Prophetically, Jesus carried His cross on His back in the same way. When they got to the top of the mountain, Abraham put Isaac on the altar and tied him there. As a father, his heart had to be broken and filled with sorrow because it was his only [legally born] son. Being 120 years old, Abraham had seen so much, that when he pulled the knife from his side, his mind had to be racing like a madman. When he lifted the knife to take his son's life, he must have closed his eyes or turned away from seeing. I know for sure he must have been praying deeply inside of his heart. When Abraham was about to bring the knife down on his son, he heard a voice from heaven. When you can't see God, perk your ears up and wait for Him to say, "Stop, I've got another way!"

Matthew 26:36 - 45 - *Then cometh Jesus with them unto a place called Gethsemane, and saith unto the disciples, sit ye here, while I go and pray yonder. And He took with Him Peter and the two sons of Zebedee and began to be sorrowful and very heavy. Then saith He unto them, My soul is exceeding sorrowful, even unto death: tarry ye here, and watch with Me. And He went a little farther, and fell on His face, and prayed, saying, O my Father, if it be possible, let this cup pass from Me: nevertheless, not as I will, but as Thou wilt. And He cometh unto the disciples, and findeth them asleep, and saith unto Peter, What, could ye not watch with Me one hour? Watch and pray, that ye enter not into temptation: the spirit indeed is willing, but the flesh is weak. He went away again the second time, and prayed, saying, O my Father, if this cup may not pass away from Me, except I drink it, thy will be done. And He came and found them asleep again: for their eyes were heavy. And He left them, and went away again, and prayed the third time, saying the same words. Then cometh He to His disciples, and saith unto them, sleep on now, and take your rest: behold, the hour is at hand, and the Son of Man is betrayed into the hands of sinners.*

Here, we see Jesus prayed with a broken heart. He was about to go through something, and the first thing He did was to pray. He demonstrated the power of praying together because He took three people with Him when He was about to seek the face of God. It shows He needed reinforcement even though they could not keep their eyes open to watch while He prayed.

## Four Results to a Broken Heart

A broken heart:
- can result in a hardened heart - difficulty in loving.
- can result in bitterness - the intention to get revenge.

- can bring on health problems - emotion expressed in our body.
- can bring on heart problems - emotion affecting our hearts' health.

## Conclusion

We don't want to go on living with a broken heart. Let's pray for healing for our broken hearts! Prayer is for those who are ready to say, "I can't do this. I need God to do it."

When we admit our own poverty, lack of resources, and helplessness, is when we are ready to let God heal us. Are you willing to let go of control? Are you ready to let God heal your broken heart? This Broken Heart Prayer is a way to, 'Let go and let God.'

> *Father, I take a stand in the name of Jesus Christ of Nazareth. I take a stand against all the works of the enemy in this situation. I claim protection for my home and family, and seal each member with the Blood of Jesus, and allow your protecting angels to surround me and them in Jesus' name.*
>
> *I call upon God for His presence to permeate the situations where my heart has been broken. Fill me with*

*the wisdom from above and for God's quick judgment upon the plans of Satan and the works of darkness.*

*I bind the power of darkness in the name of Jesus, and I send it back into the outer darkness. I call for victory in Jesus' name. In the authority of Jesus, I break the power of any curse, negative words or unbelieving prayer spoken against me. I break it off in Jesus' name and ask Him to break the power of any evil riding upon these curses or negative words. May my ears be open to God's Word, the Truth that sets me free. Feed me, Father, with Your daily bread. Speak Your very words to me. Send forth Your Words of healing and blessing, for Your Word is living, powerful and accomplishes Your purpose. In Jesus' name, I pray. Amen."*

The image of heartbreak and describing the devastating emotional pain of a broken relationship transcends culture and is expressed in the same way in almost every language. We *feel* the pain of betrayal and separation deeply at the core of our soul. It feels as if our heart really is breaking because, of course it is. God understands this experience because He has lived through a broken heart. God has been a jilted lover. Through His love for us, He has endured unfaithfulness and desertion. God understands our loneliness and identifies with us. We can talk to Him about this experience and ask Him for help at our deepest point of despair because He's been there Himself.

Brokenhearted or not, it's time to pray without ceasing. Our prayers can only be effective if we stand in agreement, forgive each other, and pray in faith. Then we will see the results of fervent prayer.

We must remember to lay aside our own feelings, forget about our troubles, focus on someone else for a change and see how our own situation gets resolved without even realizing it. As Paul said in *Hebrews 12:1-2 - Let us lay aside every weight, and sin which doth so easily beset us and let us run with patience the race that is set before us. Looking unto Jesus the Author and Finisher of our faith; who for the joy that was set before Him endured the cross, despising the shame, and is set down at the right hand of the throne of God.*

## Chapter 11

## Breaking Barriers Through Prayer

The definition of *breaking*:

1. The points at which material breaks under strain. The point at which one's endurance, self-control, etc. collapses under trial. The act, result or place of breaking through against resistance, as in warfare.
2. A strikingly important advance or discovery.

The definition of *barriers*

1. A natural formation or structure that prevents or hinders movement or action.
2. Something material that blocks or is intended to block passage.

**Seven barriers to your prayer life:**

1. Unbelief
2. Selfishness
3. Retaliation
4. Unforgiveness
5. Unconfessed sins
6. Hypocritical relationship
7. Weaknesses of the body (sleep)

This chapter will guide and assist you with the barriers of unforgiveness, bitterness, low self-esteem, pride, and fear and it will equip you with scriptures that you can directly apply to your situation. You will then be able to break through the barriers and begin to tap into your God-given inheritance and be free from bondage.

**The Spiritual War**

Ephesians 6:10-18 - *Finally, my brethren, be strong in the Lord, and in the power of His might. Put on the whole armor of God that ye may be able to stand against the wiles of the devil. For we wrestle not against flesh and blood, but against principalities, against powers, against the rulers of the darkness of this world, against spiritual wickedness in high places. Wherefore take unto you the whole armor of God, that ye may be able to withstand in the evil day, and having done all, to stand. Stand therefore, having your loins girt about with Truth, and having on the breastplate of righteousness; And your feet shod with the preparation of the gospel of peace; Above all, taking the shield of faith, wherewith ye shall be able to quench all the fiery darts of the wicked. And take the helmet of salvation, and the sword of the Spirit, which is the Word of God: Praying always with all prayer and supplication in the Spirit and watching thereunto with all perseverance and supplication for all Saints.*

This scripture is to encourage the Saints not to lose hope, exhorting them to put on all the protection they can, so that they will be able to contend with the enemy. In the commencement of his exhortation, Paul reminds them that it was only by the strength of the Lord that they could hope for victory. The word "wiles" is generally used to express deception through trickery and includes all the methods that would be part of that. It should do with cunning or skill applied to no good purpose. The devil lies to us, wants to trap us, discourage and snare us. He will do anything he can do with using his variety of cunning Satanic strategies to weaken and destroy us. He goes to work daily to produce discouragement, confusion, indifference, and imbalance. He is our chief enemy, so here is a briefing of four things to watch for:

1. The devil exaggerates the pleasures of sin while minimizing the true nature and its outcomes. The scriptures teach, (speaking of Moses) *He refused to be called the son of Pharaoh's daughter, choosing rather to suffer affliction with the people of God than to enjoy the passing pleasures of sin* (Hebrews 11:24-25, NKJV).

Observe the phrase "enjoy the passing pleasures of sin." This adversary is asking us to invest in something with the promise of immediate return without telling us about the risk, the outcome, and the ugly side! He is counting on the fact that we will see the fun and the pleasure - the joy of a satisfied appetite - and jump at the opportunity, acting impulsively. We need to stop and think, inquire, look deeply and consider the consequences. Then we will begin to frustrate devil with all his endeavors.

He wants us to act on the immediate pleasure of the tempted behavior. The bait looks good, but when you take that bite, you have taken in the ugly poison of sin. Therefore, he is annoyed when we stop to think, when we inquire about the tempted behavior, when we think in terms of long-term consequences, when we study, pray and consider if something is right or not!

2. There is an opening into our lives through our emotions - *Ephesians 4:26*. I often hear people say, "I know I shouldn't be drinking, but I was depressed," "I know I'm married, but this other woman made me feel so good," "Sure it's wrong to lie, but I was under such pressure!" or, "I know it was a sin to treat my brother the way I did, but I was so mad!"

What's happening? The devil is watching. When we fall into certain moods, or we are overcome by various kinds of emotions, the enemy steps in to defeat us and to lead us into sin. Paul said, *"Be angry and do not sin: do not let the sun go down on your wrath, nor give place to the* devil," (Ephesians 4:26, NKJV).

When I'm angry, and I take that anger with me into the next day and carry it along with me for weeks and months and years, I might as well wear a bullseye target. The enemy will find me and seek an entrance into my heart for his evil purpose and for my downfall. Use the Word of God and prayer to take a careful inventory of your moods, your emotions, and the grudges you carry. Expel the hurt feelings, the habitual and destructive thoughts you entertain and can't seem to turn loose. He can use these things to slowly erode your character, lead you into sin and gradually turn you away from God.

3. The enemy will use people to lead us astray or corrupt us. Our Lord warned to be careful about people! He knew the enemy could use people to influence us and lead us astray. So, Jesus said, *"Beware of false prophets, who come to you in sheep's clothing, but inwardly they are ravenous wolves,"* (Matthew 7:15, NKJV). When He sent His disciples out, He also said, **"*Beware of men,"*** (Matthew 10:17). The enemy can defeat us through words of invitation into sin, through false teachings or through subtle influences.

Read 1 Timothy 6:1-5. In a situation where there are teachers not consenting to wholesome words, the enemy discovers his advantage. When ministers who preach and teach, do not maintain loyalty to *the doctrine which is according to godliness,* Satan can step in through that entrance and seduce many. When we accept, endorse or consort with false teachers, that indifference plays right into the hands of error and the devil's purpose.

Let's observe how Paul described the risk to Timothy. He told him, *"From such withdraw yourself."* Too much is at stake to play around with people like this. It is one thing to be patient and kind and do what we can to work with people. But when corruption is evident and when there are those at work who are destitute of the Truth, we cannot just let error have its way.

Paul also warned the Colossians - *I say this so that no one will delude you with persuasive argument*, (Colossians 2:4, NASB).

4. Satan is a master marketing agent, he packages sin in neat, attractive bundles (Hebrews 3:12-13). What if someone came to you and tried to hand you a garbage bag? As soon as they held it out you could smell the contents, you can hear the buzz of maggots, and you can see the leaking liquids. Are you going to take the hand-off? But what if someone came to you neatly dressed in a pleasant smile and they handed you a beautiful package, like it was professionally wrapped at an upscale department store? It even has a matching bow and ribbon. Your reaction would not be the same as with the garbage bag!!

Our enemy knows how to package sin so that it looks attractive and enticing. This is part of his deceptive essence. For instance, in the lust of the eyes, he seeks to present sin to us in a neat, pretty package so that our first reaction is to look, to admire, to want, and to take.

Have you ever asked yourself what is the *real* definition of sin? Well, here's the answer - transgression against God and His Word. Simply, to go against God. There are four known ways in which a believer falls into sin, and these are:

1. Lack of knowledge.
2. Rejection of knowledge.
3. Lack of wisdom.
4. Tricked by the devil.

You are joining a battle, and we are armed to take the offensive in the confrontation. Paul warns us that we should *take all the armor of GOD to stand firm against the forces of hell* - Ephesians 6:11.

There is no room for doubt because our struggle isn't against physical forces but against invisible powers which have clearly defined levels of authority within the real atmosphere. However, Paul not only advises us of a well-defined structure in the invisible realm, but he also urges us to maintain a "combat position" against this Satanic structure. All this armor doesn't just constitute a passive protection against the enemy; it should be used as an offensive weapon.

Notice Paul's final recommendation: We should pray *all the time with all prayer and supplication in the Spirit* - Ephesians 6:18.

Thus, prayer isn't so much a weapon or even a part of the armor as how we enter the battle itself, realizing the purpose for which we have been armed. To take the armor of God is to prepare ourselves for the battle. Prayer is a battle with the Word of God as our principal weapon.

The invisible realm and the victorious war, seeing the unseen (discerning spiritual things and God's perspective) are just two of the keys to victorious prayers. The lesson that Elisha taught to his servant was that to believe the impossible, one should first see the invisible. The text speaks to us of a war between Syria and Israel where the prophet Elisha, through prophetic perception informed his people about the enemy's tactics. Prayer is the key to discern the strategies of our adversary. The panic of Elisha's servant was permitting him not to see the invisible. Notice these crucial words - *Elisha prayed!* He didn't ask God to simply do another miracle, but that He would permit him to see into another dimension. The response came immediately in verse seventeen. Seeing the invisible will enable us to discern spiritual things from a perspective more divine than humanly possible, thus glimpsing the adversary's plan of attack and perceiving the angelic force.

I believe that if we are really equipped and properly prepared, we could win each battle on every front. There are two realms in conflict, the natural and the supernatural. There are two kingdoms in conflict, darkness and light. The two kingdoms cannot rule in the same place. This is the nature of the division and conflict, not the nature of a peaceful and prosperous society. For a community to flourish, evil must be continually defeated day after day, year after year, generation after generation. Many people have become disillusioned because they feel it is a never-ending battle, but we must take heart and not be discouraged. The battle that we are engaged in will end in victory. Therefore, we must fight the good fight of faith and not doubt. We must not give in to disbelief. God's power and goodness that are within us are far more powerful than any evil outside of us. Conquer the foes of doubt and unbelief within, and our enemies outside will be vanquished. We will win over personal stumbling blocks, habits, addictions, and the struggles of injustice around the world. We long for God's will - His mercy, His salvation, His healing, and His abundance to be done on the earth just as it is in heaven. We must fight to win. This is our war.


**1. The Key to Breakthrough Prayer**
It is persevering in prayer until there is a breakthrough. We see this in the following scripture:

Matthew 7:7-8 (NIV) - *Ask, and it will be given to you; seek and you will find; knock, and the door will be opened to you. For everyone who asks receives; he who seeks finds; and to him who knocks, the door will be opened.*

It is asking, seeking, and knocking until the answer is received, found, or a door opened. It is being so persistent with getting something that we never give up until God responds. Referring to the last quoted scripture, the words ask, seek, and knock are in the present tense. We must keep on asking, keep on seeking, and keep on knocking. We are to persist in prayer.

The words receive, find, and open are also in the present tense. This shows that the answer to prayer is more than just a promise for the future. This means that those who persevere in prayer possess the answers now. Perhaps the answer has not yet transpired, but by faith, the believer knows that God has heard his prayer (1 John 5:14- 15; Ephesians 6:18).

## 2. There are Several Lessons taught by Christ about Prayer.

a. True prayer is persevering breakthrough prayer. God expects all our prayers to be persevering. When we sense a real need to pray, we not only ask, but we seek and knock. We do not play around and glibly murmur a prayer. Really pray!

b. Prayer is to be done often. Christ commanded prayer. He pointedly said: "Ask... seek... knock." And, as pointed out above, He demanded that we pray often and pray with intensity.

c. The answers to our prayers are assured (Matthew 7:9-10).
  i. God is not reluctant to give. He is not sitting back disinterested and unconcerned about our welfare. He

is as a loving father is to His children. He will not refuse the request of His dear child.

ii. God will not mock our requests. He does not give grudgingly (James 1:5). He does not even hesitate to give and what He gives is not of less quality than what an earthly father gives. God does not give ragged substitutes. He gives exactly, or better than, what we ask (Matthew 7:11; Ephesians 3:20).

iii. The things we want must be in God's will. It must not be asked from selfish desires and motives. God gives only what is good and wholesome for us (1 John 5:14-15; James 1:17, 4:2-3).

iv. True, persevering prayer acknowledges our dependence upon God. When we are genuinely in need, we come to God, to ask, seek and knock. This has been the experience of all believer's time and again. The very fact that we are asking, seeking, and knocking demonstrates that we are truly dependent upon Him.

Christ said that true prayer is a prayer that really means business. It is sincere and genuine in its requests and it keeps on asking and asking until God answers.

True prayer is not sleepy-eyed prayer, ritual prayer, routine prayer, half-hearted prayer, or doubting prayer. This is where real practical spiritual warfare is at, and most people don't even realize it. The enemy often slips in and causes the negative aspects of prayer to take place. Why doesn't God stop our adversary from interfering with our prayers? Because He has given us a free will, and He will not violate the terms of that gift because it is up to us to exercise it.

(1) *Seeking* contains the idea that we *seek* to meet the request ourselves. This is especially true if the request can be met by human effort. There certainly is no idea of sluggishness or complacency in the tone of "ask... seek... knock." The thrust is action, a *get-to-it* attitude.

(2) *Knocking* contains two ideas. First, we approach every door that we can until the right door opens. We certainly would not pound and pound away at the same door. We must move about knocking until the right door is opened.

Additionally, we must continue knocking at the door of Heaven. We must wrestle with God, not giving Him rest until He opens. Such action shows dependency upon Him. Coming to Him in fellowship and communication is bound to please Him just as such communication pleases an earthly father.

## 3. Divine Revelation

Prayer gives us revelatory perception, which is necessary to triumph in the spiritual war. In Jeremiah 33:3, God promised Jeremiah that if he called, not only would He answer but He would reveal *great and hidden things* that couldn't be understood in any other way. The word "hidden," is from the Hebrew word *batsar*, and is mostly translated as "isolated" or "inaccessible."[27] It suggests that God would give Jeremiah "revelatory intuition" by revealing things that otherwise would remain isolated or inaccessible. Such revelatory intuition has always been essential for the clear understanding of a victorious spiritual war. One can't pray effectively without a certain intuition about what to pray for and without knowing that God is truly anxious for us to seek Him in prayer.


## 4. Intimacy and Breaking Down Barriers

Intimacy with God in prayer brings blessings and victories with it. (Proverbs 3:5-6). There are two words of special significance in this passage: "recognize" and "ways." The word "ways" from the original Hebrew means, "a way, course or mode of action." It suggests specific opportunities that a person confronts continuously. The most common "portion of opportunity" that we regularly experience is each new day. This passage reminds us that we should remember God every day since He will then direct our paths.

Of similar significance is the word "recognize" (from Hebrew *yada*). In other places, *yada* is translated as "to know" with the significance of knowing through observation, investigation, reflection or direct experience. But the highest level of *yada* is obtained through "direct or intimate contact" as what occurs in marriage. Applied to the spiritual context, it suggests an intimacy with God in prayer that grants blessings and victories. By combining these ideas with our text in Proverbs, we can conclude that if we maintain *yada'* (intimate and direct contact with God) all our "days", He promises to lead us to vital and fruitful realizations.

## 5. Faithfulness in Prayer

In Acts 6:1-4, the early church quickly understood that they should pray constantly because the spiritual war doesn't stop. This idea came to be the priority just as Satan's priority was to defeat those Christians. Thus, its first administrative decision after Pentecost established the ministry of prayer (alongside that of the Word). As the church grew, issues in the church required more of the apostles' time. They soon realized that they needed more prayer rather than more activity, so they chose seven men to serve as deacons and care for the church. This initiative left more free time to the apostles to dedicate themselves more concertedly to prayer and the ministry of the Word.

Persevering in prayer is a subject which is referred to throughout the scriptures. Sometime later, the apostle Paul said to the church in Rome, *"Be kindly affection one to another with brotherly love..."* and asked the members to be *continuing in prayer* (Romans 12:10, 12).

One generation is passing on as another is being raised up. This is our defining moment. It will be the same tomorrow with the next generation of leaders. Humanity looks for a hero, and I think that many of the heroes of this generation will be unsung, uncelebrated, and maybe even unrecognized. They will be those who win battles in the confines of their prayer room. They will not fight with guns and missiles, but they will fight with the superior weapon of prayer. Now is the time to rethink how you approach prayer, so you can download God's order, regain your personal power over anti-purpose, anti-peace, anti-joy, and anti-prosperity forces, as well as reclaim the kingdoms of this world for Christ.

No one goes into to battle with the intent to lose, but battles are lost every day because the enemy we are fighting is better trained and better prepared. Prayer takes you into Heaven's boot camp and God's divine gym. Through prayer, you will quickly gain spiritual, emotional, and mental muscles. God has already assigned the greatest sparring partner: The Holy Spirit. He will prepare you for every battle you will face in life and give you divine strategies that are designed to cause you to triumph over evil every time. Consult with Him anytime you feel that you are uncertain about the nature of the battle and the appropriate weaponry you should employ.

## 6. Intercession

(Ezekiel 22:30)

The intercessor presents himself before God on behalf of others and asks for justice. It was a very sad day in Israel's history when God commanded Ezekiel to prophesy against their sins; thus, declaring that there was no other alternative but to judge the land. This chapter describes a condition so disgraceful that God himself cried, *"Enough already!"* Then the Lord makes a surprising pronouncement, which could have been avoided if only one person had come before His presence to intercede for the land. He succinctly declared, *"Search for this man!"*

The text says, *"And I searched among them for a man to stand in the gap before Me, in favor of the land."* This passage clearly describes intercession. No phrase in the scripture describes the work of an intercessor more assuredly than the phrase *before Me, in favor of others.*

It's also significant that the intercessor has another responsibility which is to be a fence. This suggests that he repairs the breach caused by the enemy, and to "put himself in place of," which means to hold off their advances.

## 7. Standards of Prayer

(Psalm 5:1-3)

Regularity and order in daily prayer are necessary to break spiritual barriers. In this text, David attempts to demonstrate this. It's significant that he used the Hebrew word *'arak* in his declaration as he said his petitions to God daily.[28] *'Arakse* is used most frequently in the mosaic writings to refer to the order of the sacrifices that should be offered to the Lord each day by the priests (Exodus 40:4). It is also used to describe an army that is organized for battle (Judges 20:20-22). Such use indicates that the "strategic order" has been prepared to enter combat. These definitions connote a well thought out order in David's prayers, a daily strategy of prayer, with a purpose and a specific intention.

## 8. Victory through prayer

(Acts 4:31-34)

Prayer brings supernatural boldness, unity, fruits, and fullness. After the healing of the lame man (Acts 3:1-6), Peter and John were ordered to cease their preaching in the name of Jesus (Acts 4:18).

They both recognized the adversity of the situation and returned to their own group of believers and then called for a period of prayer that would strengthen their faith, amplifying the dimensions of their testimony. Notice the progression of the acts that followed this prayer (verses 31-35), all of which resulted in a supernatural tremor. From this moment, more power was put into manifestation:

1. A supernatural infilling—all those present experienced the fullness of the Holy Spirit.
2. A supernatural fortitude—this prayer led to a baptism of daring courage to proclaim the Word of God (verse 31).
3. A supernatural unity—the participants of the prayer were "of one heart and one soul" (verse 32).
4. A supernatural submission.
5. Supernatural productivity - provided with a new power, they went forth prepared for God's glory (verse 33).
6. Supernatural generosity - they were baptized in a spirit of sacrifice and generosity (verses 34-35).

## 9. Physical Actions
(2 Kings 19:8-19)

Some physical actions are accompanied by the establishment of spiritual authority in the invisible realm.

King Sennacherib wrote a letter suggesting that God couldn't oppose him. Upon receiving the letter, King Hezekiah took it and presented it to the Lord in prayer (verse 14). This is an example in which a physical act seems to establish spiritual authority in the invisible realm. In other words, a physical act becomes a spiritual symbol of a reality that impacts the invisible while it is acted out in the visible world.

Hezekiah's attitude in presenting his case before the Lord represented an expression of confidence and a manifestation of the faith with which he raised his prayer. The king was convinced that God would hear his prayer. That night the Lord sent an angel to destroy 185,000 enemy soldiers (2 Kings 19:35).

Other people's physical acts recorded in scripture include vocal praise and shouts (1 Samuel 4:5-6), lifting the hands and inclining the head (Nehemiah 8:6), jumping or dancing (Psalm 149:3; Luke 6:23), laments in prayer (Romans 8:26), trembling or shaking (Acts 16:29), the intense cry (Ezra 3:13), and many occasions in which people prostrated themselves (Ezekiel 1:26-28). Impelled by faith and motivated by a genuine and intense passion for prayer, these are not superstitious actions. They treat the invisible as something real and thus, gain many victories.

## 10. Effectiveness

(James 5:13-18)

The Holy Spirit energizes the prayer of a righteous man, so that he will see results. James describes a level of prayer which is beyond the normal capacity of any believer. The prayer is strengthened by the direct participation of the Holy Spirit. The Greek word for "fervent" doesn't appear in the original text. This word constitutes an extension of the Greek word which means "effective". The Greek word *energeo* means "efficient or that which is effective."[29]

To fully understand the word *energeo,* another passage where it is used needs to be examined. Paul used it to describe the power of the Word of God, which works in a special way in those who believe (1 Thessalonians 2:13). Applied to the text, it suggests that our prayer, when it's filled with the power of the Holy Spirit, makes things happen. Our prayers themselves are effective! *Energeo* is also the source of our word "energy." It is translated as "powerful" in Hebrews 4:12 - *For the Word of God is quick and powerful.*, and "*to be mighty in*" in Galatians 2:8. Think of it as a verb meaning "to energize."

## 11. Seeking God

(Jeremiah 29:11-14)

Seriousness, intensity, and diligence are some of the things that God demands from those who pray. Throughout the scripture, we encounter numerous references to God's people seeking Him. In this passage, it is implicit that seeking God entails a level of intensity that is superior to what could be called ordinary prayer. The word "seek" along with the phrase "with all your heart" suggests an almost vehement fervor. "Seek," from the Hebrew *darash*, suggests the pursuit of a desired object.[30] It also implies diligence in the same process. In *2 Chronicles 15:2,* Azariah promises that the Lord will be with His people if they "seek" (*darash*) Him. Here we have another example of the divine emphasis on intensity and diligence in prayer.

## 12. Fasting to Break Spiritual Barriers
(Ezra 8:21-23)

A fast is a sacrificial method of prayer that achieves results.

While the exiled Jews prepared to return to Jerusalem, Ezra called on the entire nation to fast (verse 21). He encouraged them for a triple purpose - first, to ask God to guide them to *the right way.* The emphasis for this fast was directional. Secondly, they asked God to protect the children. The emphasis of this fast was help and protection. Finally, they asked God to protect their possessions. The emphasis of this fast was material.

Fasting is repeatedly mentioned in the scriptures as a sacrificial form of combative prayer, which produces results that can't be achieved in any other way. This is manifested particularly with the expulsion of demons in the time of Christ (Mark 9:14-29). The fast involves renouncing necessary sustenance while our attention is centered during this period on seeking God. A fast can last 40 days, as in the case of Moses (Deuteronomy 9:18-21), or be as short as part of a day, as in the case of David and his men (2 Samuel 1:11-12).

## 13. Angelic Activity

(Revelation 12:7-11)

God can use angels to provide victory to the Saints who participate in the spiritual war. Satan's thrust results in a great battle between the heavenly hosts and the hordes of hell. In this battle, the heavenly warriors expel Satan and his demons from the Celestial Kingdom. However, it should be noted that the victory isn't exclusively due to the angels, but that they also win using the believers' spiritual weapons. The angels battle, but the saints of God provide "the firepower." This is clearly seen in verse 11 (NLT), *"And they have defeated him by the blood of the Lamb and by their testimony."* The angels don't defeat the accuser by themselves alone; the Saints participate through battle prayers. The angels make up the means used by God to administer the victory, which is reinforced by prayer.

Notice the mention of the archangel Michael inverse 7, one of only four places in the scriptures which mentions him. In each of these references, the spiritual war is clearly implied. This is described in Daniel 10 where Michael's participation in the battle and the victory is the direct result of Daniel's fast and prayer (verses 1-4, 12-13).

## 14. Taking Authority
(Mark 11:20-24)

It's necessary to assume authority in the spiritual terrain in order to impact the natural order. Our Savior's action of cursing the fig tree indicates a passion in prayer and faith that we need to learn. When the surprised disciples later noted that the fig tree had dried up from the roots, Jesus responded with the clear order, "Have faith in God." Then when He called them to, "Order the mountain to be cast into the sea," urging them to prepare themselves for situations in which they would have to assume direct authority in the spiritual sphere to affect things in the natural sphere.

## 15. Trumpets
(Numbers 10:1-10)

Trumpets hold a unique place in proclaiming spiritual authority. The use of trumpets maintains a singular relationship with the exercise of spiritual authority in prayer. On this occasion, two silver trumpets are consecrated for the use of Israel's spiritual leaders. One was appointed for the convocation of the assembly and the other for the mobilization of the camp when they were about to begin a journey (verse two). Therefore, the first trumpet served primarily to gather the people while the second ordered the camps to begin moving, generally to go to war. In the case of the second trumpet's use, notice the words of verse nine, *"blow an alarm with the trumpets...and you shall be saved from your enemies."*

The sound of the trumpets during a victorious spiritual battle has importance for the divine plan in the end times (Revelation 8-12). All the crucial successes of Revelation 12 occur at the sound of the seventh trumpet. Later, the sound of the seven trumpets isn't heard until the prayers of the Saints, like incense, are lifted before God's throne (Revelation 8:1-6). This possibly indicates that the prayers of God's people make the seventh trumpet sound, which announces the arrival and establishment of Christ's eternal reign on earth. Hearing the unmistakable sound of the trumpet communicates to us the Holy Spirit's calling to battle (1 Corinthians 14:8).

## 16. Tears and Brokenness
(Psalm 126:5-6)
Tears of sorrow, joy, compassion, exertion, and repentance are present in spiritual warfare.

In scripture, tears fulfill a unique purpose in spiritual growth. We discover here that when tears are sown, not only is a spiritual harvest collected but it leaves a spirit of rejoicing in the sower. This passage, along with others, relates to a suffering spirit which describes various purposes and roles connected to what can be called "the ministry of tears." Charles Spurgeon defined this ministry as "liquid prayer." There are tears of pain or suffering (2 Kings 20:5); tears of joy (Genesis 33:4); tears of compassion (John 11:35); tears of desperation (Esther 4:1-3); tears of agony or labor (Isaiah 42:14); tears of repentance (Joel 2:12-13). Clearly, passion is necessary in spiritual warfare.

We know from King David in Psalm 51 that God desires a "broken and contrite heart" when we confess (verse 17). He doesn't want us to simply admit our sins and ask for forgiveness but to be sorry for them because that indicates the depth of our love for Him. David tells us how his heart was broken when he cried, *"Do not cast me from your presence or take your Holy Spirit from me,"* (verse 11).

David's relationship with the Lord was long-term and personal from the time he was shepherd boy. He knew God and had many experiences with Him. The scriptures are full of his prayers to the Lord, and the guidance and direction the Lord gave him in return. David was broken-hearted because he knew the sins in his life had interfered with his relationship with Lord, for *if we regard iniquity in our heart, He will not hear our prayers* (Psalms 66:18). David had regarded the iniquity which was in his heart; he had held tightly to his sins of adultery and murder for over a year, refusing to face them and refusing to confess them. The worst thing David could imagine was the consequence of his sins, for when he prayed, his anguish is heard in his cries out to God.

Are we broken over our sins or over losing touch with God when we fail to confess them? Brokenness is not a one-time emotion, but the result of a continuing act of our will as we confess in deepest humility and grief from our heart.

Before its impact can be felt in a home, a church, or a nation, revival must first be experienced on a personal level in the hearts of men and women who have encountered God in a fresh way. The single greatest hindrance to experiencing personal revival is our unwillingness to humble ourselves and confess our desperate need for His mercy. Our generation has been programmed to pursue happiness, wholeness, affirmation, and cures for our hurt feelings and damaged psyches. But God is not as interested in these ends like we are. He is more committed to making us holy, so that we can have full inheritance of His promises. There is only one pathway to holiness - one road to genuine revival - and that is the pathway of humility or brokenness.

## Chapter 12

### Be Anxious for Nothing

**A**nxious is derived from the word **anxiety** which is:

(1) the state of being uneasy, apprehensive, or worried about what may happen.

(2) concern about a possible future event.

(3) an abnormal state characterized by a feeling of being powerless and unstable to cope with threatening events, typically imaginary, and by physical tension, as shown by sweating, trembling, etc.

(4) an eager but often uneasy desire.

Philippians 4:6 (NIV) - *Do not be anxious about anything, but in everything, by prayer and petition, with thanksgiving; present your request to God.*

Paul exhorts us to pray about our circumstances instead of worrying about them. Philippians 2:20 (NKJV) - *For I have no one like-minded, who will sincerely care for your state* describes Timothy's concern for the Philippians. Here Paul uses the Word to refer to worry. He prohibits the people from worrying about their own problems, instead, they are to commit their problems to God in prayer, trusting that He will provide for their deliverance.

Proverbs 16:3 (NKJV) - *Commit your works to the Lord, And your thoughts will be established.*

Psalm 37:34 (NKJV) *Wait on the Lord And keep His way, And He shall exalt thee to inherit the land.*

**Commit**
    (1) To give in charge or trust: deliver for safe keeping.
    (2) To put officially in custody or confinement.
    (3) To hand over or set apart, to be disposed of or put to some purpose.

The verb **commits to** is from a word meaning **"to roll."**[32] The idea is to "roll your cares onto the Lord." Trusting the Lord with our decisions frees us from pre-occupation with our problems.

To wait on the Lord is an act of faith; not to wait on Him is foolishness. David admits that the wicked might prosper, but he also affirms that they will not enjoy success forever. As I studied the life of David, I found that he spent a great deal of his time waiting. David had to wait about fifteen years from the time he was first anointed by Samuel to the time he became king over Judah. It was another seven years before David was anointed king over all Israel. This means David waited over twenty years of his life to be made king. David's life can teach us a great deal about "waiting on the Lord." Psalm 37:9 (NKJV) - *For evildoers shall be cut off; But those who wait on the Lord, they shall inherit the earth.*

Our faith sets us towards what we have, an inner vision or desire (hope) for, and patience, keeps us going until we reach or possess that vision or desire. It was by letting the force of patience hold them on a course of faith that our ancestors came to the place of inheriting what had been promised them. We must learn how to give God charge of our lives and trust Him to make the decisions concerning everything we do or say. Once God is in charge, then there is no reason why our ways cannot be committed to Him.

When we are committed to the cause of building the Kingdom of God, He will keep us in perfect peace if our mind stays on Him. We cannot depend on our own ability or understanding for His ways are not ours. We need to allow God to take full custody of our circumstances and situations, so we can fall in line with His Word.

Even when we find that God has answered our prayers, WAIT for some more time. Sometimes there is more that God would like to reveal. Those are the things that He would reveal, further confirm and add beauty to your answered prayer. They boost our faith and reward our confidence in God. But God only reveals the rest to those who wait in prayer before Him. He reveals such things to those who do not rush out of His presence once they get the answer to prayer. Therefore, linger in His presence a little while longer; wait in prayer before Him. He has much more to tell you. He doesn't operate any faster in the twenty-first century than He did in the first. So while we rush ourselves, we can't rush God. In fact, much of life is spent waiting. While our natural inclination is to hate waiting, this period of uncertainty can actually be a time of great personal growth. Here are three reasons to wait:

(1) Recognize that God is in control, even when it seems He has forgotten you.
(2) Renew your faith in God's quiet, steady providence.
(3) Redeem your time in the waiting room of life.

When someone has custody of us, that means they are completely responsible for our whole being. Decisions should be made by them. Whatever ideas we may have will have to be approved by that individual always, not just some of the time. When we give God full custody, our entire life must be handed over and set apart. Everything that we are so accustomed to have is thrown out the door. Old habits, titles that man put on us, and religious mindsets must be changed.

Philippians 2:5-8 - *Let this mind be in you, which was also in Christ Jesus: Who, being in the form of God, thought it not robbery to be equal with God: But made Himself of no reputation, and took upon Him the form of a servant, and was made in the likeness of men: And being found in fashion as a man, He humbled Himself, and became obedient unto death, even the death of the cross.*

Once these old habits are disposed of, then we can fulfill the purpose God has for us. It's time for improvement; it's time to eliminate and let go of the baggage, right the wrongs, and make amends. No change, no promises and not even prayer can help you in this situation.

James 1:8 says that *a double-minded man is unstable in all his ways;* not some of his ways but all his ways. We do not want to be like the Church of Laodicea in Revelation 3:14-22.

Prayer is a delight, and we must delight ourselves in the Lord and stay consistent in prayer to God. The counsel of the scripture is "don't be anxious; don't worry." But we must understand that this is not saying that we are NEVER going to worry. In the Greek language, when the verb is in the present tense, it means continuous action. So, what these passages are really saying is - "Do not be continually anxious" and "Don't continually be anxious about anything." So, we should conclude that it is not un-Christian to worry from time to time, but if we worry all the time, being constantly in a state of anxiety, then we really do have to wonder about our position as a Christian. It is human to worry. That is another result of the fall of man into sin. Since we are sinners and will never reach a state of perfection in this life in the flesh, even though we are born again, it is impossible not to worry at least occasionally.


**Is God in control of the earth realm or not?**
Answer "No." God is not in control, we are in control of our thought pattern, we are in control of every circumstance in our lives. When God gave man dominion, He handed the control of the earth to us.

He gave us dominion over the inferior creatures, over fish of the sea, and over the fowl of the air.

Genesis 1:27-30 (NIV) - *So God created mankind in His own image, in the image of God He created them; male and female He created them. God blessed them and said to them, "Be fruitful and increase in number; fill the earth and subdue it. Rule over the fish in the sea and the birds in the sky and over every living creature that moves on the ground." Then God said, "I give you every seed-bearing plant on the face of the whole earth and every tree that has fruit with seed in it. They will be yours for food. And to all the beasts of the earth and all the birds in the sky and all the creatures that move along the ground—everything that has the breath of life in it—I give every green plant for food." And it was so.*

If you can recall all the events you've been anxious about over the course of your life and how they turned out, was all your distress justified? Did it affect the outcome? Did it accomplish anything? Were you able to reach the goal that you set for self? Rationally, we all agree that worry isn't good for us. So why do we keep doing it? Because God being invisible, it's hard for us to remember that we need to invite Him into our situation. That is why He created prayer.

He's waiting for us to ask Him. How much easier life would be if we could see God moving things around, putting people and circumstances together, working out our problems for our ultimate good. But there is something else at work, and it is us. If we're completely honest, we should admit that we have been in control for so long that we forget that there is a God who we can come to no matter the time.

Everybody worries - even people who should know better. Take Jesus' twelve apostles for example. They became afraid when a storm overtook their boat. Jesus was so unconcerned about it that He was happily fast asleep. They fretted that there wouldn't be enough to feed the five thousand and in the most heart-rending account of fear in the New Testament, the disciples were so distraught that they would be arrested after Jesus' crucifixion that they hid in a locked room. If anyone should have been able to trust Jesus, it should have been these eyewitnesses.

The Apostle Paul found his strength in God. He reminds us that, II Corinthians 11:23-12:10 - *I have… been in prison… frequently, been flogged… severely, and been exposed to death again and again. Five times I received from the Jews the forty lashes minus one. Three times I was beaten with rods, once I was stoned, three times I was shipwrecked, I spent a night and a day in the open sea, and I have been constantly on the move. I have been in danger from rivers, in danger from bandits, in danger from my own countrymen, in danger from Gentiles; in danger in the city, in danger in the country, in danger at sea; and in danger from false brothers... I have known hunger and thirst and have often gone without food; I have been cold and naked... Who is weak, and I do not feel weak? Who is led into sin, and I do not inwardly burn? If I must boast, I will boast of the things that show my weakness... I will not boast about myself, except about my weaknesses... [God] said to me, 'My grace is sufficient for you, for My power is made perfect in weakness.' Therefore, I will boast more gladly about my weaknesses, so that Christ's power may rest on me. That is why, for Christ's sake, I delight in weaknesses, in insults, in hardships, in persecutions, in difficulties. For when I am weak, then I am strong.*

According to the Bible, there is nothing wrong with realistically acknowledging and trying to deal with the identifiable problems of life. To ignore it is dangerous and wrong. It is also unhealthy to be immobilized by excessive worry. Such worry must be committed to praying to God, who can release us from paralyzing fear or anxiety and free us to deal realistically with the needs and welfare of others and of ourselves. **If you are a constant worrier, fill your spirit with the Word of God.**

BE MORE REALISTIC - many people are worried and anxious about events that will never actually happen to them. Relax. Focus on today. Take life one day at a time.

ACT - If there is something practical and wise that you can do, then do it to alleviate the problem or avoid needless danger. Don't put it off; procrastination will generally raise your anxiety level.

TALK to someone. Don't hold all the anxiety inside. It can be a big relief to share your fears and worries with someone else - a friend, relative, pastor or counselor. If fear and anxiety are an ongoing problem in your life, schedule a regular time each week to talk with someone who can walk you through the Word of God. The Bible is the road map to your recovery.

It is true that Jesus was in anguish when He was praying to His Heavenly Father prior to His arrest - so much so that His sweat was tinged with blood. This condition is called hemosiderosis and happens only in severe anxiety which causes the body to release chemicals that break down the tiny blood vessels in the sweat glands. Having the foreknowledge of what was going to happen to Him, it was quite normal for anxiety to overwhelm Him. Luke 22:44 - *And being in anguish, He prayed more earnestly, and His sweat was like drops of blood falling to the ground.*

However, notice how Jesus dealt with His anxiety - *Father, if You are willing, take this cup from Me; yet not My will, but Yours be done* (Luke 22:42, NIV). He brought all His anxiety to His Heavenly Father and abided in God's will. The results were astounding *an angel from heaven appeared to Him and strengthened Him* (verse 43).

Jesus suffered like this so that He would be able to identify with our suffering. He knows exactly what we are going through and is willing to come to our aid.

## Chapter 13

# Overcoming through Prayer

**O**vercome - to get the better of something; overcome difficulties; to gain the superiority: to win.

*Revelation 21:7 - He that overcometh shall inherit all things; and I will be his God, and he shall be my son.*

The Greek word "to overcome" is N*ikao*, means victory over hostile powers; to subdue something or to prevail over something.[33]

An overcomer is a conqueror, a winner or a victor. This victory has its foundation on the victory already won by Jesus Christ. He is the real conqueror, winner and true overcomer! Thus, the only way we can become overcomers ourselves is when we yield everything to Him and allow Him to conquer, subdue and prevail through us.

Overcomers are those faithful and obedient Christians who not only "talk" about doing the will of God but who actually "do" it. As Matthew 7:21 says, *not every one that saith unto Me, Lord, Lord, shall enter the Kingdom of heaven; but he that doeth the will of My Father which is in heaven.* By doing God's will, these believers can overcome the world, the flesh, and the devil.

Remember David in the Old Testament? He was an overcomer, and yet remember all the ways he blew it! The New Testament, however, calls him, *"a man after God's own heart."* Why? Because David knew how to confess his sins, how to turn around after committing them and then go God's way. This is the kind of "overcomer" we are to become.

David not only fought for the kingdom, he defended it, he built it, he increased it, he inherited it, he worked it, and he stayed connected to the kingdom. So, we must know our identity in the Kingdom, who we are connected to, what we are connected to, and why we are connected to it. We must know our position and the place we are to be in the Body of Christ. One of the places I choose to take in the Body of Christ is praying, which allows me to overcome all obstacles.

Psalm 51 is a soul poured out prayer before God with great transparency and brokenness of spirit. It is marked by true characteristic repentance such as:

- Appeal to the mercy of God
- Honesty
- Understanding of the severity of sinning against God
- No excuses or justification
- Desire to reform
- Recognition that forgiveness is not deserved but by grace alone.

We can see one way to overcome is by praying and confessing and turning away from what we have become accustomed. David showed us the examples as to how Christians can overcome anything that they may face. In verse two of this chapter, David asks God to do three things:

1. He asked that his sin be blotted out, which speaks of human records which can be erased.

2. He asked to be washed thoroughly, which compares forgiveness to the washing of clothes, and clothes were often seen as an extension of the person.

3. He asked to be cleansed from his sin, and this refers to liturgical ceremonial law. David wished to be separated from his sin in every way possible. He's not clinging to it with secret affection, but he is rejecting his sin to uttermost, which allows him to overcome.

For those who have *not* been obedient or faithful in their walk with the Lord in this lifetime, they are justified but *not* experientially sanctified. They are nominal, lukewarm and backsliding Christians (believers who once had "fruit" in their lives but who have decided not to make the choices needed to stay in God's will). They have quenched God's Spirit in their hearts. They, in fact, have been *overtaken* by the world, the flesh and the enemy. They have left their prayer life and chose some other kind of lifestyle instead of holding onto the Rock that is higher and stronger than we could ever be.

There will be two kinds of inheritance - one is an inheritance that belongs to us simply because we are "sons" of God (it's called a sonship inheritance). This is a gift that all true Christians enjoy and one that allows us to *enter* the Kingdom freely. The second type of inheritance refers to a meritorious reward that only overcoming Christians will receive for their obedience, faithfulness, and endurance. This reward will allow us to inherit the Kingdom (or have an inheritance "from the Lord"). These are the ones who not only will be *subjects* in the coming Kingdom, they will also be co-rulers with Christ. Believers in Him need to be positionally sanctified so we can be partakers of Christ's life.

We don't want to make *emotional choices* to follow our own desires rather than God's. It will cause our individual hearts to be quenched and blocked thus, we are now operating in our own thoughts, emotions, and desires. 1 Thessalonians 5:19 - *Quench not the Spirit.*

If we continue *not* to recognize that we have quenched God's Spirit and we never choose to turn around and repent, we will ultimately end up fruitless. This will deem us unfit, unprepared and unqualified to inherit the Kingdom. When a believer makes "faith choices" to continually turn around and follow God, they are the ones who have denied themselves (the flesh) and have chosen to let Christ's life come forth (that beam of light). They then become partakers of Christ's life, and overcomers who produce fruit. The beam of light does not always flow however, it comes and goes, depending upon their choices. But these "overcomers" have learned how to recognize when they quench the Spirit and how to let Christ, who is the perfect One, live His life out through them.

I want to share one of my personal testimonies of obedience and how I overcame. By September 2009, I was already living in

Orlando with my only child Sashoi. During a visit to her doctor, she was diagnosed with Chronic Lymphocytic Leukemia. When she got the news at the doctor's office, the first thing she did was to call me. She was crying so hard she made me cry too, and I did not even know why she was crying. I told her to stop crying and let me know what is going on. She shouted out, "I have cancer!" I said, "Cancer? What are you talking about?" She said that they wanted to admit her right away and that it was all in her blood. I immediately said to her, while still on the phone, "Calm down. Go ahead and do what they tell you, and I will be there." I turned to my supervisor and told them what was going on, and they told me I could leave. After I had arrived at the hospital, I told her to be quiet and not to accept anything the doctor says; just trust God and He will see us through.

My daughter contacted our First Lady from our church and explained to her what was going on. At that time, I was also working on an upcoming prayer conference entitled, "The Power of Praying Together." The enemy fought me in my mind - it was a battle I knew I must win. The enemy said, "Now you can't go through with the prayer conference!" I chose not to listen to what he was telling me, instead I was determined to go through with it no matter what. Then the Holy Spirit stepped in with this verse of scripture, Philippians 3:13-14 - *Brethren, I count not myself to have apprehended: but this one thing I do, forgetting those things which are behind, and reaching forth unto those things which are before, I press toward the mark for the prize of the high calling of God in Christ Jesus.* Suddenly, I felt the strength of the Almighty God like fire shut up in my bones!

It was then I remembered a prophecy that was given to me about a year before. An Evangelist came up to me and said, "This thing that your daughter is getting ready to go through is not unto death but for the glory of God." I did not understand what she was talking about at the time, but I kept it at the back of my mind. This was the hope I had to hold onto. I proceeded with the prayer conference, and it was a remarkable success. Let me share with you the underlined titled of this prayer conference, just to show you how this was supernaturally orchestrated by God. This was the title Holy Spirit gave me and the different inserts included on the flyers:

*The Power of Praying Together: Friday, September 25 – 6:30 p.m. and Saturday, September 26, 2009 – 8:45 a.m.*

*God is calling us to proclaim the Gospel and demonstrate by His Power the works of His Kingdom. This conference is for those who really want to "bring in the Kingdom" to their jobs, schools, homes, and communities.*

*That if two of you shall agree on earth as touching anything that they shall ask, it shall be done for them of My father which is in heaven. Matthew 18:19*

*This conference will challenge you, inspire you and equip you. Each day will provide opportunities for prayer experiences to heal emotional woundedness and physical needs. There will be revelation knowledge to empower you for evangelism, healing, and spiritual warfare. This conference focuses on the ministry of healing prayer, based on the life and ministry of Jesus, believing that His mandate given in Luke 4:18-19, is also the calling of the Church today.*

God moved supernaturally in the conference, and my daughter still proceeded with her chemotherapy. Her first treatments went well without any problems, and while she was in the hospital, my First Lady came up to me and said, "God said she would live and not die – just continue to declare the works of God!" I turned to her and thanked her for those words. This was truly a divine act of God. Even I did not realize it until it was upon me. **The power of prayer and preparation is the key to answered prayer.**

This was one of the most humbling times of my life. I did not talk much, and I just found myself worshiping God every moment I got. Worship was my focus; I could not do anything else. I remember saying to God, "I don't have the desire to pray right now; all I want to do is to worship You and give You glory." I had peace like I had never experienced. It was peace I could not explain. Then, in October of that same year, my daughter went back to work a week and a half after her first treatment. The swine flu outbreak had started, and my daughter's job was at center where a lot of kids with disabilities attended. So, with the outbreak of the swine flu, so she had no idea what she was walking back into.

A few days after going back to work, she started coughing quite a bit. I kept saying to her, "Baby, I don't like the way you are coughing so please call your doctor and have them check you out." As a concerned mother, I kept on her, and by the end of the week, things took a turn for the worse. I drove her to the hospital and dropped her there and told her, "I will be back. Go ahead and get checked in, then make sure you tell them everything you are feeling. Also, please make them aware that you are undergoing chemo." I don't know why she said this to me before I drove off, but the words she said bothered me a little. She said, "Mom, the same way I walked in this hospital on my two feet, I will be walking out of here the same way."

It was a Saturday afternoon on October 10, 2009, when I took her to the hospital when I was scheduled to leave for Texas on the following Monday to attend a strategy conference. I went back to the hospital later that evening before I went to work. During my visit, she was breathing heavy and seemed to be short of breath to the point where they had to put the oxygen mask on her to help her with her breath. They advised me that they were running several tests so that they could rule out the swine flu. The first test came back negative, but she seemed to be getting worse by the minute.

I left and went on to work because there was nothing I could do for her now except to trust God. While I was at work around 9:30 p.m. that night, she called me screaming on the top of her lungs saying, "Mom, I can't breathe, and they are not trying to help me!" I told her to put the nurse on the phone. I asked the nurse what was going on, why was she screaming so hard and why is there no one helping her. She explained that she was panicking because she can't breathe, and it is causing stress on her body. I told the nurse to put her back on the phone, then spoke gently to her, telling her to calm down and allow the nurses to do their job. They eventually had to give her some medicine for her to calm down. The next day, which was Sunday after church, I went by the hospital, only to see her in a screened off room. I had to now wear a mask and overalls before I went go in the room. The doctors explained that even though the test came back negative the first time, they are treating her for the swine flu virus and were retesting to see what the next result would be.

Finally, the second result came back and it was positive. They started to give her double the antibiotics. I went back on Monday to visit her before I boarded the plane and when she realized that I was going to leave, she started to hyperventilate because she did not want me to leave her. But I heard the voice of God saying in my spirit, "You must go."

I prayed with her and assured her that God was with her and she would be alright. I gave instruction to my best friend, Latonya, to make sure she took care of my baby until I got back in town.

While I was sitting on the plane, my phone rang, and Latonya said, "I am at the hospital, but they won't let me give her anything to eat, because she has taken a turn for the worse, and they may have to put her under oxygen, so that she doesn't overwork her lungs." I told her let them do whatever they had to do, just keep me updated.

The plane got delayed for about an hour, and I called my First Lady and updated her what was going on. I remember saying that I had no idea what do, whether I should get off the plane or stay. While I was talking to her, I heard that still small voice again, "You must go," and believe you me I was not going to disobey the voice of God. Then I remembered Philippians 2:8 - *And being found in fashion as a man, He humbled himself, and became obedient unto death, even the death of the cross.* This was my moment to obey God, so I stayed on the plane.

I arrived in Texas and checked into my hotel room around 6:00 p.m. and around 8:00 p.m. my phone rang. It was the doctor. He said, "Miss Tinson, your daughter's heart just stopped, and we had to resuscitate her, and her right lung just collapsed while we were trying to remove air from the pleural space between the wall of the chest cavity and the lung." All I remember saying to the doctor was, "Do what you need to do to save her."

I hung up the phone and looked up to heaven and said, "God you said she would live and not die, so her life is in your hands." I then went in the bed and drifted off to sleep. The peace of God was so evident in me - I could not explain it. Philippians 4:7 - *And the peace of God, which passeth all understanding, shall keep your hearts and minds through Christ Jesus.*

The phone rang the next morning around 8:00 a.m. It was Latonya telling me she was on her way to the hospital. I said to her, "When you get to the hospital, the only thing I want to hear is *it is well*. I don't want any details of her condition; just tell me *it is well*." Her response was, "Ok, I will."

She got to the hospital, and after her visit, she called me around 10:00 a.m., and said, "It is well." I told her, "Thank you." We talked for a few minutes and said, "Goodbye." This was on Tuesday, my second day in Texas.

I relaxed around the hotel that day until it was time to go the evening service at the conference. When I walked in the conference facility, I could feel the presence of the Holy Spirit hovering all over the room. There was prayer going on, and the anointing was so strong I could feel every hair standing up my head. One of the Bishops' Pastor was leading the prayer that evening. What an anointing! During all this, I could hear the Spirit of Lord just ministering to me and consoling me. I almost felt like someone was carrying me and I was just floating in the air.

After the worship service had ended, it was time for Bishop to speak. From the moment he got on the platform, the Spirit of the Lord was so strong on him. He said, "It's time for miracles to happen!" For about thirty minutes, he spoke only about miracles. He gave a testimony about a young boy who was on his deathbed and how God healed him. At that moment, I felt like God was talking to me. I felt that this whole service was appointed just for me. No one could tell me anything else. I just knew that God had this time set aside just so He could personally minister to me. I knew it was not an angel, but it was the Holy Spirit Himself who was ministering to me on a personal level.

I heard the Spirit of the Lord say, "I got your back. I promise I will never leave you. You gave yourself over to me for others and I want you to know I remember your sacrifice. I remember you crying to Me on behalf of others. So, what makes you think that I would leave you now?" Then *John 14:1* came to mind - *Let not your heart be troubled: ye believe in God, believe also in Me.* I whispered back to Him and said, "I believe, and I trust You with all my heart." It was almost like I could see this big smile on His face. Even while I am writing this testimony, I can still see that smile. I can't explain how I could see the Spirit of God smiling, but I just did. It is an experience like no other.

During the conference, there was a lady who had never met me before. She walked up and handed me a piece paper. When I read it, I was amazed at what it said, "I came that you might have life and life more abundantly." It also had several scriptures on the miracles of healing, and all I could do was to smile and thank her. I kept that pink piece of paper for a long time because it had just what I needed for that specific time.

I made a special request to God. I said to Him, "When I go home, I want to see my baby awake." That was all I wanted because, during this time, the only thing I could do was to worship. I never asked God why, I never asked anything. I just trusted that He knew what was best for me. All I wanted to do is to draw closer to Him, closer than I'd ever been because *He was wounded for my transgression, bruised for my iniquity and the chastisement of my peace was upon Him and by His stripes, we were healed.* (Isaiah 55:3). That was the Word I had to stand on and nothing else.

For the entire week of the conference, God ministered to me, and I felt that comfort and had the confidence that I could endure hardness as a good soldier. I would reap the good of the land, and I did. I got back to Orlando that Saturday afternoon and went straight to work that night. Some might say, "Why you didn't go to the hospital first?" Well, I was just being led by the Spirit of God.

Nevertheless, Latonya who was being "mama" during my absence went with me to the hospital that Sunday afternoon. I could not face it alone and she knew that I needed someone that would have my back. When I got to the hospital, the sight was unbearable, more than anyone could stand. She was hooked up to everything you could imagine, tubes going everywhere. I could feel the tears rolling down my cheeks, but I knew I had to be strong, and not break down. Latonya kept on talking to her and stroking her arms, and she told her, "Your mom is here," and then I saw tears rolling down my baby's face. I knew then she was still in that body. Then a few minutes later, she tried opening her eyes, and I could see her hands starting to move. The monitor started to go off because she was getting a little anxious, so the nurses had to sedate her, and wanted her to rest for a while, so they suggested that I come back the next day.

I was back at the hospital the next morning. She was asleep, so I tapped her and said, "Mommy is here." Her eyes popped open and she attempted to write because she couldn't talk - her hands were so weak. She was determined not to give up, and by the end of that day, she was writing better.

By Tuesday, they had moved her out of the critical ward to continued care. By the end of the week, she was walking around; and two days later they released her from the hospital. The doctor admitted that this was a miracle and there was nothing else they could do but trust God. My daughter is alive and well now, and there's no trace of leukemia in her body. We overcame by the blood of the Lamb!


**What are the Requirements for Inheriting?**
One of the most frequent questions asked is, "What do we have to do in order to be *worthy* of inheriting from the Lord?" Specifically, what does Matthew 10:38 really mean when it says: *He that taketh not his cross and followeth after Me, is not worthy of Me?*

## "Worthy"

There are two Greek words for the word "worthy" and they are very important for us to understand. The first one is the Greek word *kataxioo* which means to be *counted worthy*; to be deemed entirely deserving.[34] We are *counted worthy* only because of what Christ has already done for us on the cross. He has redeemed us, imputed His righteousness, and gave us His holiness. In other words, He is the One who is worthy. We are only *counted worthy* because of what He has already done. Luke 21:36 validates this - *Watch ye, therefore, and pray always, that ye may be accounted worthy (kataxioo) to escape all these things that shall come to pass, and to stand before the Son of Man.* So according to this verse, all true believers in Jesus Christ (the faithful) are *accounted worthy* to escape the things to come and to stand before the Lord!

The second definition of *worthy*, is the Greek word *axios* which means *to be worthy of; on the grounds of being fit; meet or prepared*.[35] In Revelation 3:4 where Christ is talking about the church of Sardis, He says - *Thou hast a few names even in Sardis which have not defiled their garments; and they shall walk with Me in white; for they are worthy.* This is the kind of *worthy* that we are talking about in relation to inheriting the Kingdom. It means being fit, prepared and qualified to rule and reign with Christ, holding levels of responsibility.

Here's a list of some of the specific things the Bible says we need to attend to so that we may be considered *worthy* to inherit the Kingdom.

1. We need to learn:
- How to be experientially sanctified or conformed into Christ's image (Romans 8:29).
- How to give Christ the complete rights to our lives, daily.
- How to submit to His Absolute Lordship.
- How to be set apart for Him (1 Thessalonians 4:3).
- How to be clean and open vessels (Ephesians 5:1-5).

2. If we do sin or when *self* does raise its ugly head, we must learn how to go to the cross, repent and deal with those things. Unless the cross is a constant part of our lives, we will not experience Christ's overcoming life. John 12:24-25 tells us that life only comes from death (death of our "self- life").

3. Next, we must learn:
- How to be a partaker, a participant and a sharer of Christ's life (Hebrews 3:14; 12:10). Not just a receiver of His life, but living and experiencing His life.
- How to love others with His love (2 Peter 1:3-4).

- How to produce the "fruit of the Spirit" (Galatians 5:22-23).

4. Finally, we need to learn *how to overcome the world, the flesh and the enemy by being obedient, faithful and persevering in prayer to the end* (Revelation 21:7). You see, I became worthy to receive the supernatural healing power of God through my faith in God. Sashoi's result was the manifesting power of the Almighty God through faith, believing, receiving, and overcoming. We must remember He is supernatural and only works in the supernatural.

**Promises to the Overcomers**
Chapters two and three of Revelation speaks extensively about overcomers. It is to these overcomers that the "blessings" of the future Kingdom are assured. Read some of the incredible promises God makes to these overcomers:
- They will be clothed in white (Revelation 3:5).
- They will be "pillars" in the Lord's temple (Revelation 3:12).
- They will be granted power over the nations (Revelation 2:26).
- They will enjoy the tree of life (Revelation 2:7).
- They will not be subject to spiritual death (Revelation 2:11).
- Their names will be acknowledged by Christ (Revelation 3:5).

- They will be fed out of the hidden manna (Revelation 2:17).
- They will have a white stone with their name on it (Revelation 2:17).
- Christ will write His own name upon them (Revelation 3:12).
- They will sit with Christ on His throne (Revelation 3:21).

The real reason for our calling is to rule and reign as kings and priests with Christ in the coming millennial kingdom and after that, for eternity. Genesis 1:26-28 and Revelation 5:9-10 are two scriptures that confirm we were created for this very purpose. Thus, everything in the universe moves toward this goal. Being conformed into His image is critically important. Most Christians acknowledge the millennial kingdom to some degree or another, but many have no idea as to what is required to enjoy a significant role there. There are many scriptures that talk about the requirements for ruling and reigning.

II Corinthians 5:10 talks about the judgment seat of Christ and tells us that *all* Christians will be judged according to what they have done, either for good or for bad. This judgment is a judicial evaluation. It's here that our position in the coming Kingdom will be determined. So, this judgment seat is *not* just for rewards! Rewards have more to do with levels of responsibility that will be given to us. When we become more like Him, we will be qualified to share with Him in the inheritance, and to work with Him in important positions of high responsibility over the whole universe. *Effective faith is more than just belief.* It's more than just knowing the scriptures and just going to church on Sundays! Saving faith is learning how to be a partaker of Christ's life, which means not only receiving His life at our new birth, but also living His life every day!

The Bible calls these kind sanctified Christians *overcomers.* The Lord promises some incredible things to these overcomers - *He that overcomes shall inherit all things; and I will be his God, and he shall be my son* (Revelation 21:7). If you haven't already, take a moment to read Revelation 2:1 through Revelation 3:22, which talks about the Seven Letters to the Seven Churches. This passage of scripture was given to John by Jesus, not only about seven existing churches at that time but also about all churches in general and each of us individually. In other words, these letters are written to all churches of all ages and all individuals in every age.

The "rewards of inheritance" that are promised to each of these churches and to the individuals in them who overcome, apply to all of us. Consequently, we need to listen carefully to what Jesus is saying because each of the rewards He gives correspond to the exact measure of faithfulness the believer manifested in his life. It's important also to note that seven times in these letters to the seven churches, Jesus says (through John), *"I know your works."*

In other words, Jesus is emphasizing *works* in these letters. In fact, in Revelation 2:26 He says, *He that overcomes and keepeth My works unto the end, to him will I give power [authority] over the nations.* Here, again, Jesus is talking about the millennial kingdom, and He is stressing a special kind of *work* that a believer must do – "My works." He is talking about the things that are done *by the Holy Spirit* through us. He is not referring to the works of the flesh but to the works of the Spirit.

**The Seven Churches of Revelation**

Let's take a moment then to look at who the overcomers are in each of these seven churches, and let's pay close attention to what God promises them in return for their faithfulness, obedience, and endurance. Remember, these letters are addressed not only to churches in general but to each of us individually!

1. *Ephesus* (Revelation 2:1-7) - Ephesus represents the *apostolic church*, which endured great hardships, but God said He knew their "good works," their labor and their patience. These saints were strong on doctrine, but they had forgotten and forsaken the most important thing - their first love which is that special intimacy with the Father. He then exhorts them to repent.

God's promise to the faithful and obedient overcomers in the church at Ephesus was that they would eat of the "tree of life" which symbolizes being equipped with a special wisdom and knowledge for the future Kingdom.

This tree of life first appears in Genesis where it says *man was created to rule and reign* with the King of Kings over all the earth (Genesis 1:26-28). Then, it disappears from the earth because man was not able to rule and reign with Christ. But in Revelation, it shows up again in the millennial kingdom as man will once again be able to co-reign. So, the "tree of life" will have some significance with our future inheritance in the millennial kingdom.

2. Smyrna (Revelation 2:8-11) - Smyrna represents the persecuted church or the suffering church, whose elders said they were Jews, but were not. Some were Jews in name only. God tells this church that He knows their poverty and their suffering, but He promises them if they are faithful and obedient unto death, He will give them the crown of life (James 1:12). Interestingly enough, this is one of two churches that has nothing negative stated about it.

God's promise to the faithful and obedient overcomers in the church of Smyrna was that they would not be hurt in the *second death*. The second death - where death and hell are cast into the lake of fire - comes at the end of the millennium and involves unbelievers at the White Throne of Judgment. Because of their perseverance, even unto death, God promises overcomers a victorious crown.

3. *Pergamos* (Revelation 2:12-17) - Pergamos represents the church that was married to the world (Constantine's era). As God puts it, these are the ones that *"dwell where Satan's throne is."* This church had allowed the evil doctrine of Balaam (which represents monetary gain by compromise) and the doctrine of the Nicolaitans (corruption of delegated authority) to infiltrate the church. God exhorts them to repent.

God's promise to the faithful and obedient overcomers in the church of Pergamos was that they would eat of the *hidden manna* (divine physical provision for the future) and receive a "white stone," which is a victory stone for Christians whose works endured the fire. This stone will have a new name written on it that no one knows, except the one who receives it (Revelation 2:17).

4. *Thyatira* (Revelation 2:18-29) - Thyatira represents the Orthodox Church where the evil spirit of Jezebel could reign. You might want to read about Jezebel, the patron of Baal

worship, in 1 Kings 16:30-34 and 21:25 because in the end times, this spirit is said to return. The goal of the spirit of Jezebel was to (and will be to) seduce God's faithful servants into disobedience and fornication. As John phrases it, Thyatira hit the *"depths of Satan."* In verse 22, God is going to cast Jezebel and her followers into the great tribulation unless they repent. Therefore, God exhorts the faithful to "hold fast" till Christ's return. He says they shall also receive the "morning star," which means they will have a special relationship with Jesus Himself (Revelation 22:16). They will shine like the Lord, reflecting His brightness and glory.

God's promise to the faithful and obedient overcomers in the church of Thyatira is that they will have authority over the nations and rule them with a rod of iron (speaking of the millennial kingdom).

5. *Sardis* (Revelation 3:1-6) - Sardis represents those in the denominational church who say they are alive, but who really are dead. The Spirit tells them that if they don't wake up, He is going to come *"like a thief in the night,"* and they won't even know it. Their name tells us they are alive but in reality, they are dead. God exhorts them to be watchful and repent and strengthen the things which remain. There is nothing good said about Sardis.

God's promise to the overcomers in this church is, *"Thou hast a few names even in Sardis that have not defiled their garments, and they shall walk with Me in white, for they are worthy"* (verse 4). The word *worthy* here is the Greek word *axios* meaning, to be worthy on the grounds of being fit, prepared and qualified to reign with Christ in the coming Kingdom.[36]

The white raiment must do with the wedding garment for which Revelation 19:7 states that all of us are now supposed to be preparing for ourselves. It speaks of the internal preparation we must continually do to produce the fruit of righteousness which God desires. It's not enough to just put on surface cosmetics, we must allow the Lord to complete the inward beautification process (conformity to His image) that will ultimately produce the fruit He is looking for.

6. Philadelphia (Revelation 3:7-13) – Philadelphia represents the church that had endured patiently.

Revelation 3:7-13 records Christ's message to the sixth of the seven churches addressed in *Revelation 2–3*. The Philadelphian church is the recipient of this letter. Philadelphia was a city in Asia Minor (modern-day Turkey) on the Imperial Post Road, an important trade route.

The message is from the Lord Jesus Christ through an angel or messenger, likely was directed to the Pastor. This was not John's personal message to these believers; it was a message from the Lord, who identifies Himself as, *"Him who is holy and true, who holds the key of David. What He opens no one can shut, and what He shuts no one can open."* This description of Jesus emphasizes His holiness, His sovereignty, and His authority. The reference to the key of David is an allusion to the Messianic prophecy of Isaiah 22:22. Jesus is the one who opens and shuts, and no one can say Him nay.

Jesus affirms the church's positive actions - *I know your deeds. See, I have placed before you an open door that no one can shut. I know that you have little strength, yet you have kept My Word and have not denied My name. (Revelation 3:8).* The church of Philadelphia was weak in some respects, yet they had remained faithful in the face of trials. Because of this, the Lord promises an opening of blessings.

Jesus' letter then condemns the enemies of the Philadelphian believers - *I will make those who are of the synagogue of Satan, who claim to be Jews though they are not, but are liars - I will make them come and fall at your feet and acknowledge that I have loved you. (Revelation 3:9).* Those who persecuted the believers (the persecutors were religious hypocrites in this case) would one day realize Christ loves His children. The church of Philadelphia would be victorious over its enemies.

7. *Laodicea* (Revelation 3:14-22*)* - Laodicea is the church with the lukewarm faith. The seventh and final letter to the churches of ancient Asia Minor is to the church in the city of Laodicea. Laodicea was a wealthy, industrious city in the province of Phrygia in the Lycos Valley.

The message is from the Lord Jesus Christ via an angel or messenger (likely a reference to the church's pastor): *"To the angel of the church in Laodicea write . . ."* (Revelation 3:14). As with the previous messages, this was not simply John's message to those in Laodicea; it was a message from the Lord. Jesus identifies Himself thus: *"The amen, the faithful and true witness, the ruler of God's creation."* These titles emphasize the Lord's faithfulness, sovereignty, and power to bring all things to their proper completion (the "Amen").

## Chapter 14

### Faith Mixed with Prayer

I found out that if I wanted my prayers answered, I didn't just send up a list to God as though He was the great Santa Claus in the sky. There were some things which were required from me. I had to get my life cleaned up and get on the right track. I needed to be reading the Word of God and living in obedience to His Word. The good news was that I didn't have to make it all happen by myself. The Holy Spirit would teach me all things and enable me to live the way I should. Understanding the Holy Spirit was the key to seeing the power of God move in response to my prayers.

Let's use the power of prayer and compare it to the engine of a car. There is very little power in the key that fits my car. The car engine has power, but it does not come to life without the keys being put into the ignition. In other words, I don't have the power to go outside and get myself going sixty miles an hour, but I have access to a resource that can get me moving at that speed. Jesus said in Matthew 16:19 - *I will give unto thee the keys of the Kingdom of heaven.* This key means authority, privilege, and access. The key represents your faith, the ignition represents the Word of God, and the engine represents God. Once faith moves in prayer, then we get God to start moving in His power that's in His Word. Some things will not be turned on unless you turn them on. Some things will not be turned loosed unless you turn them loose. Some things will not be set free unless you set them free. The key doesn't make the power of the engine, instead it releases the power of the engine.

I understood that having legal possession of the keys to a car was evidence that I have the right to that car. In the same way, because Jesus gives us the keys of His Kingdom, we have the right to come before God in prayer. John 1:12 - *But as many as received Him, to them He gave the power to become the sons of God, even to them that believe on His name.*

Having the keys to the car also means that we have the responsibility for it. Matthew 16:19 continues... *And whatsoever thou shalt bind on earth shall be bound in heaven: and whatsoever thou shalt loose on earth shall be loosed in heaven.* We are responsible for our side of the partnership with God in prayer. If we don't use the keys to prayer, then nothing is likely to happen. There won't be anything released or unlocked.

Our problem is we sometimes forget where we put the keys to our car. The same is true in our prayer life. We misplace the keys that unlocks God's power. We come upon a situation, or a situation comes upon us, and we forget to use our ability that is already given. Whenever I lose the keys to my car, I ask God to show me where they are and help me to find them. He always does. Whenever we lose sight of our prayer or faith, we can ask Him to help us find it again, and He will.

**Starting the Engine**

Keys serves no purpose if we refuse to use them to unlock the item they were created to unlock. If the car's key doesn't connect with the ignition, the power of the engine will not be ignited. God's power is always available to us, but if we don't use the key of prayer, faith, and belief, we can't appropriate this power for our lives.

Have you ever wondered why there are good people who love God, read His Word, and pray, but they don't see His power move in response to their prayers? Why their lives don't affect or change the world around them for His Kingdom. As a result, the world looks upon their faith as being irrelevant. This happens because there is a misunderstanding of the need to ask for the Holy Spirit's power.

The precious Holy Spirit enters every believer, but He only moves in power in those who invite His overflowing enablement. Those who don't invite Him are like cars that have fuel in the tank, but the engine has not been turned on. People often hesitate to pray because they do not understand the power of the Holy Spirit working through them when they do, or they don't believe that God's power is there for them. Too often we think the power of prayer is not attainable for the average person. But God says it is available to all who love Him with their whole being and love others as themselves.

There is an important correlation between God's love and God's power. John 13:34 - *A new commandment I give unto you, that ye love one another; as I have loved you, that ye also love one another.* If you're going to function as a person of the Kingdom, then there are certain regulations you need to observe. The foundational law of the Kingdom is the law of love. It's not a casual feel-good-ism. It is the love of God poured forth in our hearts. Romans 5:5 - *And hope maketh not ashamed because the Holy Ghost, which is given unto us, sheds the love of God abroad in our hearts.* The fountainhead of all power is that flow of the divine love of God happening in us. Loving others is a Kingdom law, and you can't get Kingdom action without obeying Kingdom laws. His keys don't fit our private kingdom. His power is unleashed upon command but not our personal gain.

It doesn't mean we don't benefit from His power; we certainly do every day whenever we acknowledge that we need a fresh flow of God's power working in us and ask for God's Holy Spirit to flow through us as we pray. We will then see His power move in our lives however, He wants us to recognize that His Spirit is love. If we want a demonstration of God's power, then God's love must be the motivating force behind everything we do and each prayer we pray.

To move into that kind of love-motivated praying, our first step must be to submit ourselves to God and wait at His feet in prayer. Like I said earlier, it is not that He is keeping His power from us, He just wants us to depend on Him for it. He wants to ensure that we get everything we need for the journey ahead.

We cannot go forth until we have the necessary clothing that prepares us for what lies ahead, because we must first look at our nakedness. We cannot pray without being clothed in God's power. Then we wonder why we don't get our prayers answered. It is one thing to be clothed with the righteousness of God through the blood of Jesus Christ, but we also need to be clothed with power for being what we were created to be on this earth. We are to be clothed with the armor of God for spiritual warfare. God is saying that He doesn't want us going naked into the world that needs us to be prepared with what is necessary for us to make a difference.

John 5:2-9 - *Now there is at Jerusalem by the sheep market a pool, which is called in the Hebrew tongue Bethesda, having five porches. In these lay a great multitude of impotent folk, of blind, halt, withered, waiting for the moving of the water. For an angel went down at a certain season into the pool, and troubled the water: whosoever then first after the troubling of the water stepped in was made whole of whatsoever disease he had. And a certain man was there, which had infirmity thirty and eight years. When Jesus saw him lie, and knew that He had been now a long time, in that case, He saith unto him, wilt thou be made whole? The impotent man answered Him, Sir, I have no man, when the water is troubled, to put me into the pool: but while I am coming, another stepped down before me. Jesus saith unto him, Rise, take up thy bed and walk. And immediately the man was made whole, and took up his bed, and walked: and on the same day was the sabbath.*

How did these people get to the pool, to begin with? Someone or something had to bring them to that spot. Some were blind and needed to be led, and the crippled need to be carried. The Bible did not say anybody put them in the water - they had to step in which is by moving or acting. A blind person moves according to sound, a deaf person according to sight or feelings, and a lame person moves by crawling or sitting down and pulling themselves. The central theme here is that *you* must act. If I am in debt up to my head, I must mix prayer with my faith and move in faith. Here are the actions: First, I must get a better paying job to contribute to the reduction of the debt and secondly curb my spending or use of debt. I have now positioned myself in a place to be blessed and for my debt to be wiped out. I must move in the natural for the supernatural to take place.

**The Importance of the Word of God in Faith**

The secret of getting God on the scene and working on behalf of humanity must do with His Word given forth by the power of the Holy Ghost. He says concerning His eternal word - *So shall my Word be that goeth forth out of My mouth. It shall not return unto Me void, but it shall accomplish that which I please, and it shall prosper in the thing whereto I sent it* (Isaiah 55:11). The angel told Mary that no Word of God shall be void of power (Luke 1:37).

Jesus even said - *Heaven and earth shall pass away, but My Words shall not pass away* (Matthew 24:35). The scriptures also declare that God watches over His Word to perform it. *In the beginning was the Word, and the Word was with God, and the Word was God*

(John 1:1). God spoke the words that compiled together formed the scriptures or His Holy Word. He is behind every Word and in every Word. He watches over every promise to make it good.

Jesus said *if thou canst believe, all things are possible to him that believeth* (Mark 9:23). He even affirms that, *without faith, it is impossible to please Him* (Hebrew 11:6). If we can only get faith into our hearts and into the hearts of those who need help, then God's Word will work in ways beyond what we can imagine.

**Where does Faith come from?**
And how can we get it? The scripture teaches us, *faith cometh by hearing and hearing by the word of God (Romans 10:17).* If you don't have faith, you can get faith to come to you and live in your heart. If you have friends who are because of their lack of faith, be sure to share with them how they too can activate their faith in the same way.

What makes faith arise from the throne of God and walk, run, or fly into our lives and produce the mighty works of God? We have already established that it comes by hearing the Word of God! You won't be able to see God's work without faith because it comes only through the Word. There can be no salvation, no healing, no miracles without faith which comes from hearing, receiving, and acting on the promises in the Word of God. The secret is to speak the Word of God to others.

Once the Word is presented, it should take effect in their hearts, which will then produce faith. Then when faith arises in their hearts and the promises are received then acted upon, God moves to back up His Word, and the supernatural takes place. The only thing God has promised is to confirm is His Word! The Lord was working with His disciples and confirming the Word with signs and wonders (Mark 16:20). God works only in relation to His Word. When He wanted to redeem mankind, He sent the Word, and the Word became flesh in Jesus. If we are too indifferent to study the Word, we cannot expect results. We may talk, reason, weep, fast and pray, but unless we work out the Word of God, faith cannot come or accomplish anything. Psalm 126:6 says, *He that goeth forth and weepeth, bearing precious seed* (the Word of God) *shall doubtless come again with rejoicing, bringing His sheaves with him.*

**Individual Faith**

A person must have faith in his own heart for his own deliverance! Jesus said to the blind man - *Go thy way; thy faith hath made thee whole* (Mark 10:52). To the woman who was healed of the issue of blood, He said - *Daughter thy faith hath made thee whole* (Mark

5:34). He said to the two blind men - *According to your faith be it unto you* (Matthew 9:29), and they were healed.

If you need help, then you must have faith. If your friends or relatives need help, then they must have their own faith. Notice the order of what Jesus did. He first preached and taught the Word of God, then He healed the sick. The scripture teaches that Jesus went about preaching and teaching, and then healing all manner of sickness and diseases among the people (Matthew 4:23). He honored the Word, then preached the Word, and so must we.

Faith can only be released where the will of God is known. We will only have what we can believe we can receive when we pray. God needs our permission and participation to get involved in our lives. Boldness in faith is born out of the trust that we have in the faithfulness of God. It is at the time of challenge that the enemy attempts to steal our faith. When operating in faith, we should never make decisions based on our abilities, but on God's Word. Faith can change our lives' resume. Faith can be a greater or lesser degree in our lives at any given time. The more we know of God, the more of the His promises we will be open to experiencing.

It takes the same process of faith to believe for something big as it does to believe for something small. Faith is not magic but a systematic spiritual process that brings to pass the will of God.

It took faith for me to adapt to change. It was a difficult time in my life when I decided to obey God and move to the church I currently attend. I went there with my own beliefs and my own doctrine, which I thought was of God. When I was challenged by my pastor to start walking according to the Word of God, the internal fight began. It was a do or die moment for me; I was full of religious beliefs, not even knowing how to work the Word. I was in turmoil. A part of me wanted the change, and another part of me did not want to submit to this change. Then one day, the Holy Spirit suddenly nudged me with Romans 7:23 - *But I see another law in my members, warring against the law of my mind, and bringing me into captivity to the law of sin which is in my members.* Then I remembered that I need to pray and seek God for His help to rid myself from self-righteousness, rebellion, disobedience, and to help me renew my mind.

I must say it did not happen overnight, but gradually the change began to take place, bit by bit. Sometimes, the enemy raised his ugly head, and I had to keep confessing the Word over my mind to keep it subject to God's will. I fought with my pastor for years, rejecting everything he was trying to instill in me because of past experiences (personal, physical and spiritual). But nevertheless, he never gave up on me. He just stood his ground, and because he did, I have so much respect for him. This book would not be possible if it was not for this man of God who decided not to move an inch and let me have my way. Thank you, Pastor Alan Newman. He also introduced me to an awesome Bishop named I. V. Hilliard. He is integrity at its best; if there was ever another word that I could use to describe him, I would use it. When I visited his ministry, I learned some steps to faith mixed with prayer.

**Four Reasons Why Faith is Important:**

1. It pleases God.
2. He rewards those who diligently seek Him by faith.
3. All of His promises are received by faith.
4. We overcome every circumstance and situation by faith.

**Three Things Happen when I use my Faith:**

- God respects it.
- God responds to it.
- God rewards it.

**Eight Steps to Exercising Faith:**

1. Find the promises in the Word.
2. Make a choice to believe God's Word.
3. Sow the Word into your heart.
4. Keep your thought life in agreement with the Word.

5. Release faith by speaking His Word.
6. Corresponding actions: act like the Word.
7. Offer the sacrifice of praise to God continually.
8. Wait patiently for the manifestation.

**Four Ways to Rest in Your Faith**

1. **R**-renew your mind towards your situation.
2. **E**-endure the temporary condition, knowing it lasts only for a little while.
3. **S**-stand on God's Word until the promise manifests.
4. **T**-trust God for the end results because He is your Deliverer.

**Change, Growth and Desire**

1 Peter 2:1-3 - *Wherefore laying aside all malice, and all guile, and hypocrisies, and envies, and all evil speaking, as newborn babies, desire the sincere milk of the word, that ye may grow thereby: if so be ye have tasted that the Lord is gracious.*

What is your desire? I know it's God's desire that He should be first and foremost. His desire of accomplishment of our assignments for each person individually can be different because we all have different assignments and are made uniquely, yet in the image and likeness of God.

We all can agree that growth is a good thing however, growth requires change. Change is hard for most people, but truth without change makes growth is impossible. If you are not willing to change, you cannot grow. Most people fight against change, especially when it affects them personally. For example, how many of you have ever been in a setting where someone comes up with a great idea? Then someone bursts out, "But, we've always done it *this* way?" Well maybe that's true, but sometimes there is only one way to know if the idea will work, it is by moving toward that change.

I read a quote by Leo Tolstoy where he refers to the fact that everyone thinks of changing the world, but no one thinks of changing themselves.[37] This is a very profound statement. What we find ourselves doing all the time is that we want to change everything around us instead of letting Jesus Christ change us. We always want to change the world before we change ourselves. We must strive to be the change agents in our world, but we must have grown first in our own lives. The ironic thing is that change is inevitable; it's going to come whether we like it or not. Look around for a moment. Are things the same as they were five years ago? The answer is, no. We are living in a day where things are so advanced we can't even keep up with the changes that are taking place in just this country alone, not to mention around the world. Change is inevitable, but emotional and spiritual growth is optional.

How many people have we witnessed who are completely resistant to change? We choose to grow, or we can fight it. Just know that if you are unwilling to grow, you will never reach your potential. God's desire for us is to fully achieve from glory to glory. It is our responsibility to receive His Word, precept upon precept.

My pastor has said repeatedly that the way we were last year, is not where we are today. We can change the location of the church or our job and even the clothes we wear. We see people change churches because they did not like what was preached. Once their feathers got a bit ruffled, they ran, but what they did not realize is that was their opportunity to embrace change and cultivate growth. They made a choice not to grow. When we don't think we need to grow, then I guess we must have already arrived and we don't need to make any type of adjustment in our lives.

Making the change from someone being an occasional learner to someone dedicated to personal growth is very difficult. Don't become like the quarter Sunday church-goer. They don't ever pray or open the Bible except on Sundays. They are not committed to personal growth. If they were committed to personal growth, they would be in the Word every day and not just when the preacher gives the sermon on Sundays.

Look at a two, three or four-year-old child and see how hard it is to get them just to sit still or focus on something longer than a few minutes. It is a challenging task, but it can be done. During their lives, they will grow physically and intellectually. It goes against the grain when people choose not to grow or when they want to stay where they have become comfortable and familiar.

People celebrate when they graduate from school, and they will say to themselves, "Thank goodness that is over. I don't have to study anymore or open my books anymore." But that type of thinking doesn't take you higher than average. The moment you stop growing is the moment you start dying. There is no stagnation in God, you are either going one way or the other. If we are going to grow in God, we must learn how accept change.

We started out by talking about *wherefore laying aside all malice, and all guile, and hypocrisies, and envies, and all evil speaking,* emphasis on *all*. Not just doing away with these behaviors only when you feel like it, or when it is convenient, or even when things are not going your way, but *all* that means everything.

*As newborn babies, desire the sincere milk of the word that ye may grow thereby.* Are you a babe in Christ? A lot of us think it's about our time in the service of our Lord, however, that is not what the Word teaches. If that was the case, God would not have made an eight year old boy a king. It is not about our age or our time in service - it's about what is happening in us. Do you look the same ten years ago as you do now? With age, you are going to change. None of us look like babies anymore; some of us have more hair, some have less, and some have grown wider and some shorter. So, there it is proven again, change is inevitable, but growth is optional.

## Three Things to Encourage Growth in God

1. The first place you must start is with your desire. What is the desire of your heart? And don't use the generic statement, "I want to be closer to God."

2. How do you desire to do that specifically? Well, the Word gave us the answer in 1 Peter 2:1. We must check ourselves. When we do fall short of what God expects of us, we must immediately repent and not allow the sin to grow. Stop watering the sin in your life.

3. When we see someone living out of the will of God, we automatically know the love of God is not in them, so we don't have to talk about it or even try to show them up. Just know the love of God is not there.

1 John 2:15-17 - *Love not the world, neither the things that are in the world. If any men love the world, the love of the Father is not in him. For all that is in the world, the lust of the flesh, and the lust of the eyes, and the pride of life is not of the Father but is of the world. And the world passeth away, and the lust thereof: but he that doeth the will of God abideth forever.*

In other words, you are going to be consistently growing. You might not grow overnight because it is a process. Physical growth takes you through the steps of growing and developing daily. It is the same way the Body of Christ must progress both individually and collectively.

# Chapter 15

## Delight Yourself in Prayer

Delight means to take pleasure in something or someone, to have joy or enjoyment. Desire means to earnestly long for the possession of some object. Desire is the product of association. We can think of it in this manner - He is a loving Father who desires a relationship with His children and He takes great delight in them. For one to delight himself in the Lord, we must have a deep desire for the things of God. He gives us the desires of our heart. He has set the criteria for our desires. He will only give you those desires that are in line with His Word.

There are three criteria for our desires, and these are;

      1. Life

      2. Godliness

      3. Enjoyment

There are three types of desires, namely:

1. Godly
2. Carnal
3. Sinful

If we are going to be a part of building the infrastructure and bringing the vision and mission of a ministry to pass, it must become a complete desire of every individual in the house.

*Psalm 37:4 Delight thyself also in the Lord; and He shall give thee the desires of thine heart.*

The word "also" is an adverb which means something else is added before or after just like it. So, to understand why the writer said, *"delight thyself also,"* you must go back to *Psalm 37:3 - Trust in the Lord and do good; so shalt thou dwell in the land, and verily thou shalt be fed.* So, we can't delight ourselves in God unless we can first trust in Him. Before we can confess verse four back to God, we must be sure we are following the verse that comes before it.

Trust is to have confidence, reliance, dependence, and faith in something or someone. When you say you trust someone, you totally depend up on them and rely on their every word, which allows you to be depended upon them. Your faith is completely locked into their words.

The NKJV version of verse three states - *Trust in the Lord and do good; dwell in the land, and feed on His faithfulness.* If you continued reading out loud, to yourself and hear the words that are being repeated back to you, even in verse *5-7*, you will be able to see if you meet the requirements to delight yourself *also* in the Lord. Now take a step back, and see clearly why your desires are not met.

What is hidden in our hearts? Hidden means to conceal or camouflage something that is real to you. Because it is so real, you can never see yourself being in the wrong. No one can correct you because everyone else is wrong, and only you are right even though your perception may be so way off. Now you must take the opportunity to let *Romans 12:2* work for you, or you will only be left up to your reprobate mind. Try to be more open-minded and look objectively at what others are trying to propose and watch what God can do. Allow the Holy Spirit to bring light on the things that are festering in your heart.

If evil intention is in your heart, no matter how good your words sound, nothing good can come of it. Let's look at an evil thought for a moment. I am going to use giving since that is one of the things most of us struggle with. When the church asks for certain financial help, some of us right away think and even speak out loud, "Where do they expect us to get all this money from?" or, "Why do they just keep asking for money?" Those are evil thoughts. Then we begin to compare our last church we attended with the current one, and the first thing we say is, "When I was at the other church, I never had to do all of this giving." But what we don't realize is that the other church may have been much larger, and so you were never pushed to go beyond the norm.

With God, normal is never good. Normal means we are just average, and we should not just want to be average. I am talking about delighting ourselves in the Lord. How can we delight ourselves when we are just average? No light can shine on that. The scripture says that *a corrupt heart brings corrupt thinking, and corrupt thinking brings corrupt speech or words.*

Look at the phrase *a good man*. The word *good* simply means that this man may be better than most, so that he can bring forth upright things. Did you ever wonder why we probably remain the same? Sometimes we get to an emotional place where there may be too many evil thoughts running around inside our heads - too much negativity, then all we can show for it is barrenness and deadness. It's time we get rid of the dead spirit, so life can come to the Church. Could it be that we are stopping the flow and the move of the Church? Who are we really delighting ourselves in?

If God shows us something concerning a ministry as to why it is not growing, the reason why He would show us is because He is expecting us to do something about it. If we cannot do anything to change the circumstance, then just stop complaining about it and let the Spirit of God work to change the situation. Our job is to pray and seek the face of God or, if we are in the position to change it, then do it with our whole heart. There is no point in God showing us anything if we can't change the situation - He would be just wasting His time. This allows change to work in us. If we are not affecting change, let us be careful of our idle words because they can cause us to be judged.

We don't want is to end up like the Pharisees and Sadducees. The Pharisees and Sadducees were two prominent groups in Judaism during the time of Christ. Both groups claimed to be true followers of Judaism, but their beliefs were considerably different. The Pharisees were primarily associated with the laymen of Israel. In doctrine, they held not only to the Law of Moses and the prophets but also to a whole body of oral tradition. Their activities were centered in the synagogue.

On the other hand, the Sadducees were associated with the priestly caste for which worship was centered in the temple. Extremely conservative, they based their beliefs essentially on the Pentateuch - the five books of Genesis through Deuteronomy *(see Acts 23:6-*

*10).* When there are too many differences of opinion, it can cause dissension in a congregation. Where there is confusion, no delight and no desires are being met. John the Baptist warned them of the wrath to come while he was preaching in the wilderness. He also warned them of the wrath to come, and urged them to bring fruits meet for repentance *(Matthew 3:7-8).*

*Fruit* in this scripture means giving back something to God that will meet the repentance requirement. It also represents something that is constantly bringing life and continually growing. A fruit offering can be souls that we bring to Christ which brings continual growth to the ministry.

When we take a deep look at ourselves and consider our ways, we may find at times that we are not lining up with the Word of God. We hit and miss every time. We must take pleasure in the things of God and begin to move according to the Word.

Do you ever wonder why we take the hard road instead of just obeying the God's Word? One second we will vow to worship and serve the Lord with our whole hearts forever, and then the next second we become selfish beings, following our own paths. Many times, the Lord must discipline us so that we will look to Him (once again) and desire to serve Him. But why not just obey and avoid the chastisement? To become bitter towards the Lord during chastisement is to mock the fact that the Lord Jesus Christ loved us enough to die for our sins. Hebrews 12:6 (NKJV) - *For whom the LORD loves He chastens, and scourges every son whom He receives.* It later goes on to say that chastening is not pleasant at the times but yields the peaceable fruit of righteousness! Just as we must discipline our children, so the Lord must discipline us (a lot) in our Christian walk!

Many believers become bitter when they disobey the command of God, and as a result their prayers don't get answered. Then they blame it on God and say, "I don't see anything working for me", and "The Word of God is not true." But unruly children don't get rewarded for being bad, they simply get punished. Ask David. He demonstrates that disobedience can bring separation from the Spirit of God. Above things I do not desire, it is to be separated from the Spirit of God. It is just not a good place to be.

I know this from experience. In 1992 things seemed to be great in my life. I had an excellent job and was making good money, living in the best apartment, and driving the best car. I had one foot in and one foot out of the church. I did what I wanted to do. I was in and out with God like He was my buddy. I did not have a relationship with the Holy One of Israel and did not understand who He was or what He was about. As I continued spiraling downwards, every now and then I would give myself a little time to relax, and I would hear the Holy Spirit nudging me. *Jeremiah*

*26:13* would come up before me - *Therefore now amend your ways and your doings, and obey the voice of the LORD your God; and the LORD will repent Him of the evil that He hath pronounced against you.* I would ignore that voice and kept on doing what I wanted to do. Then suddenly one day, a shifting came with the company where I worked. They changed management companies, and suddenly I was left without a job. It was such an immediate shake-up, I could not even focus on my day-to-day activities.

When the new management took over, they gave us notice and told us we would have to leave within two weeks and they gave us a little severance which was not enough to survive. Before I knew what was happening to me, everything fell under my feet. I had nothing on which to hold on to. I was a mess and started to blame God for everything. I did not even want to pray anymore. The more I rejected the Spirit of God, the worse things became, and I fell into self-pity. The, "Woe is me", attitude did not change my circumstances but instead, only made it worst. I was left without a job, then little by little, I begin to lose things. My car got repossessed so that I could not even go looking for a job.

I continued this way for months, and then I started using my 401K money to survive and caught the city bus that only ran by the hour.

Then that money started to run out and finally, I decided to go sign with a temporary agency. They sent me on an assignment to work at a bank for $7.50 an hour. I almost fell off my seat when the representative told me how much they were paying. I thought she had lost her mind and was joking, so I had to ask just to make sure I had heard correctly, "How much?" Unfortunately, due to my situation, I had no choice but to accept it.

I started to work with the bank from 4:00 p.m. to midnight. No buses run past 11:00 p.m. I had to make some friends at work, put my pride behind me, and ask a young lady to give me a ride home. She agreed. Somehow silently I spoke under my breath and said, "Thank you, God."

One day, while we were driving, the young lady started telling me that she goes to church but she is not really saved, but she knew it was God who touched her heart to give me a ride. She had asked if I was a Christian and I shook my head, "Yes", but did not go into too much detail. After I got home that night, I felt a deep guilty conviction. There was also something wrestling with my spirit. I knew what it was. It was the Holy Spirit trying to get my attention, and I fought with myself until I fell asleep but could not get any rest. Then I heard a very angry voice in my sleep shout loudly, *"Luke 13!"* I turned over and was so scared that I was shaking. I took the Bible and open to *Luke 13* and started to read. It was a little confusing to me at first, and I started asking myself, "What do I need to repent about?" I reached down to *verse 3 - I tell you, Nay: but, except ye repent, ye shall all likewise perish.* I could not shake this verse at all, and it stood out the most in the whole chapter. Then I my spirit started to stir. I could no longer resist. I fell to the ground on my knees, and I began to cry out loud to God, and I repented of my ways, and the Spirit of God consoled me. It was something I'd never felt before, and then that small voice whispered, *"You are forgiven; now wipe your tears, and get back to being who you were, and not who you are trying to be."*

I shared this testimony, so you don't have to walk that road, but stay in the will of God and obey His every command. Get lost in His presence and in His Word, so you can be a delight to Him. Chastisement is not pretty or comfortable, so try to avoid it at all costs. Having the Holy Spirit living in us is essential to how we can delight ourselves in the Lord. When we are filled with the Holy Spirit, and in constant fellowship with Him, we are less prone to becoming spiritually tired or burned out. We are taught to walk in the Spirit. This is a personal, private fellowship with the Him that others do not see. However, the results of it are seen in the passion we have for righteousness and the things of the Kingdom of God.

The anointing is a supernatural impartation that gives us the divine ability to accomplish things we could not accomplish on our own. I could not have accomplished repentance on my own, I needed the Holy Spirit, to help me accomplish this task. Here is a sample prayer to invite the Holy Spirit to come and dwell in our hearts:

*"Father, in Jesus name, I long for You! Come and quench this thirst in me! Yes, Lord! I come to You in the name of Jesus asking You to fill me with Your Holy Spirit. According to Acts 2:17, You have promised to pour out Your Spirit upon all flesh! We are living in our last days. I claim this promise and plead for Your Holy Spirit Lord! Your Word says, 'Whatever we ask we shall receive!' Let Your Holy Spirit step into my heart, Lord, and let His mighty presence engulf me even now, in the name of Jesus. Lord, wash me thoroughly from every iniquity and cleanse me of all my sins and shortcomings so that Your Holy Spirit can dwell in me.*

*"Dear Lord, unless Your Holy Spirit comes into my life, I can never live a flawless life before You. I need Your Spirit now. Open my heart to You and take control of my whole being and quench this thirst. Thank You for granting me this precious gift. Let Him be my sweet companion forever and let Him direct my steps according to Your Word. Let Your will be done. I know You have heard me and have answered this prayer because I ask this in the most precious name of my Lord and Savior Jesus Christ. Amen."*

Getting close to God is not as hard as we make it to be. For many years, I tried running from Him. Have you ever had a best friend or a new boyfriend in your life, and all you wanted to do was spend time with that special person? That is all you need to do with God. We need to treat Him like we would our best friend or that special person in our lives. When we make time to spend with Him, *we* get blessed tremendously.

It took me many years to get to that place. Don't let it take you twenty or thirty years before you make up your mind and get close to Him. I thought I was making a sacrifice by getting close to Him, but when I took an inventory, it was not a sacrifice at all. It takes commitment and when I finally did, I realized that I loved spending time with Him. Spending time with Him, makes our minds clearer and our day goes smoother. When we go to bed and when we wake up, let's take the time to say, "I thank you, Lord, for this day."

I start my morning at 3:00 a.m. That's the time I feel I get the morning glory, and it seems I can hear much clearer. Be sure to allow some meditation time, in order to be able to hear from Him. Be quiet and still, because this is the time when the Holy Spirit will give His instructions. The presence of God can be so strong that time really doesn't matter because all you want to do is stay there.

You may ask the question, "What if I don't have the time to spend so I can experience this intimate moment with God?" Time doesn't matter when it comes to God. We live in a physical world with its four known space-time dimensions of length, width, height (or depth) and time. However, God dwells in a different dimension—the spirit realm—beyond the perception of our physical senses. It's not that God isn't real; it's a matter of Him not being limited by the physical laws and dimensions that govern our world, therefore He has the ability to miraculously redeem our time.

Knowing that God is a Spirit *(John 4:24)*, what is His relationship to time? You can find the answer in *Psalm 90:4 (NIV)* where David used a simple yet profound analogy in describing the timelessness of God - *For a thousand years in Your sight are like a day that has just gone by, or like a watch in the night.* The eternity of God is contrasted with the temporality of man. As believers, we have a deep sense of comfort, knowing that God, though timeless and eternal, is in time with us right now. He is not unreachably transcendent, but right here in this moment with us. He's in the moment with us so He can respond to our needs and prayers.

Our lives are but short and frail, but God does not weaken or fail with the passage of time. So, make the time and get out of the microwave mentality and get in the presence of God and allow Him to transform your spirit, mind, soul, and body.

Let us try not to box God in. He cannot be kept in a box framed by our own intellect. No matter how busy our lives become, make the time to sit and talk with the Spirit of God. Jesus left Him as our guide. Let's use the tools that have been given to us because tools that go unused will get rusty and hard to function, then you will have to find some type of substance or oil to saturate it for it to become functional. Remember this one thing - *For the vision is yet for an appointed time and it hastens to the end [fulfillment]; it will not deceive or disappoint. Though it tarries, wait [earnestly] for it, because it will surely come; it will not be behind, on its appointed day (Habakkuk 2:3).*

## Chapter 16

## Developing a Prayer Ministry

In order to have an effective prayer ministry, we need the following: personal relationship, purpose, passion, priority, power, principles, and consistent practice.

These elements must be adapted daily in order to **plan, prepare** and **promote** a successful prayer ministry team.

It is then that we will begin to see an increase in participation and the development of passion within others to meet with God through prayer, resulting in praise to our Lord. Most of us don't plan anything before we decide to call a prayer meeting. I believe planning is one of the most effective ways of getting anything done. Planning allows you to be prepared and be ready for any obstacle you may encounter. Engaging in organizational planning and working to implement change can be a difficult, daunting and unpredictable process. Leaders often wonder where to begin, what to take into consideration, how to overcome resistance, and how to ensure the changes made will be successfully. Here are a few tips when preparing to build a prayer ministry.

**Evaluate and Build on the Prayer Group's Strengths**

- Assess areas for improvement to enhance and see results
- Analyze the environment surrounding the group for trends and opportunities
- Examine internal and external barriers to the success of the prayer organization's strategic vision
- Determine how current you are with answered prayers to change or to support a specific strategic direction
- Gather pertinent information from key players within the group or organization
- Communicate with each other, whether they are internal or external prayer partners

## Personal Relationships Produce Results

If prayer is going to be real and meaningful to people, then they must understand the foundation and essence of fervent prayer. It is more than attending a meeting - it is more than just making our request known to God. It is connecting with our heavenly Father. It is more than a programmed event or activity - it is coming into the presence of the Almighty God. It is more than a Christian discipline - it is communicating with a living and personal God. Remember in Luke 11:1-4, when one of the disciples asked Jesus to teach them to pray, He said to them, *"When you pray, say: Our Father ..."* Jesus was teaching them the personal and intimate nature of prayer.

We are to make our prayer meetings or prayer efforts about the relationship, not merely prayer requests. Words are shallow and meaningless when there is no sense of connection. When God Himself is the main attraction, you won't need gimmicks or arm-twisting to keep people coming or interested in the power of prayer because as II Corinthians 3:17 states, - *Where the Spirit of the Lord is, there is liberty, freedom and the ability to walk in the power of the Almighty God.*

## Being an Example of Having a Lifestyle of Prayer

- In conversations, ask the person if they would like you to pray with them immediately about what was just shared. Soon there may be other pockets of prayer around the church as people follow your example.
- When someone e-mails a prayer request, let them know that you will be praying for them as you reply. You may even type out your prayer or part of it in the e-mail.
- As you hear or watch the news, silently pray for the current events right then and there, or ask those in the room to join in prayer.

When teaching, use illustrations when appropriate. Use examples referring to times when God led you to stop and pray. Watch as others grab hold of that idea for their own lives.

## Maintaining the Right Purpose for Prayer

In developing a prayer ministry, the objectives need to be established so that team members will understand the goals for the ministry. It could be that one of the objectives is to see God take care of a whole list of prayer requests, or possibly to see Him do great and mighty things. Perhaps as the originator of the group, you simply want to be obedient to His command to pray. Whatever the reason, keep in mind that team members will undoubtedly find a greater level of effectiveness when their purpose is centered more on God than any other reason for meeting.

As stated before, don't judge people based on their eloquence or lack thereof. If people sense that they may be judged in these ways, they will shy away from praying aloud or may not want to be a part of the group. Have a sense of awareness in the group and even when calling a prayer meeting, be sensitive to the Spirit, watch and pray.

## Development of Discernment

**Cultivating the Passion for Prayer in Others**
Teach and preach in a way that people are presented with God as the great God He is. This will help them to understand His ways, which will give them a good foundation of His Word. By so doing, they will help develop faith, perspective, and discernment that will grow their passion for meeting with Him in prayer. A passion for prayer stems out of a passion for God.

Keep the purpose of prayer ever before the people. Take great care that prayer doesn't become routine or ritualistic, vary the approach.

Even Jesus warned against vain repetition. Matthew 6:7. says we should pray with *all kinds of prayers and requests.* Be careful not to get into a rut. Keep your approach fresh, so you don't become dull or desensitized in praying.

**Prayer must be a Priority**

- Specific time must be set aside for prayer no matter what else is going on. During the stress and trials of life, we need to pray more, not less. The title of Bill Hybel's book, *Too Busy Not to Pray*, says it well. In both our private lives and in the church, we can let the concerns of this world crowd out our communion with God.[38] So often in prayer meetings, we can spend so much time on preliminaries or sharing prayer requests that we have little time for actual praying. Token prayers are usually shallow without much passion. Here are some tips to help to get creative in how to present prayer requests, and handle preliminaries in order to save time and allow more actual prayer.

- Have people write their requests on note cards or slips of paper. Put them all in a basket and pass the basket around for people to choose a request randomly.

- As people arrive have them write their requests on a transparency white or chalkboard and keep it displayed as you go into prayer. Announcements could also be handled this way.
- Collect prayer requests by email or phone throughout the week and type up a list to distribute. People can then pray using the list.
- Share requests in groups of three and then have only one person from each group pray for all the requests of their group in the larger setting.
- Structure the meeting's time into segments of prayer with a brief time in-between to share something about that segment.
- Incorporate praise for answered prayers.
- Build follow-up into the structure. One possibility is to have people journal prayer requests and answers they have seen. Brief sections of what they wrote could be read or compiled and then distributed.

Be careful of not making praying to come across as a passing fad or following the latest church movement. Prayer needs to be the norm, as the expected response in all situations. When prayer is a pattern, we do not just come together for prayer in times of need or crisis. As seen in the example of the early church (Acts 2:42), we will be devoted to prayer wherein we promote a prayerful environment and not merely a prayer meeting.

**Planning Strategies for Effective Corporate Prayer.** Church leaders can pursue the relational aspect of prayer, understand its purpose, be impassioned, view prayer as a priority, know its power, adhere to scriptural principles, and make it a personal practice in their own lives, but still not have a praying local church body. Why? How can that be? The reason is not for lack of tactics.

**The Reason may be a Lack of Strategic Planning.** Notice the adjective before planning - strategic. Having effective corporate prayer is not just a matter of scheduling meetings or developing a program. To truly be a church of prayer is to be able to engage in spiritual warfare. What nation would go into battle without carefully planning their strategy? To do so would undoubtedly lead to failure.

**They Assess their Situation.** Your plans need to be tailored to where your people are NOW. Do not expect your people to take a giant leap in their perspective, passion, and priority on prayer. Winning the battle over prayerlessness is a process that comes out of growth. What it takes for your group to get there will not necessarily be the same that worked in another church.

**Train your People.** Having assessed your situation, you know the strengths and weaknesses that contribute to the potential success of your mission to become a people of prayer. Begin where the body is, then take them to the next level. Lay the biblical foundations. Impart the vision. Model the life of prayer. Zero in on what is missing - personal relationship, purpose, passion, priority, power, principles or permanent practice. Be patient with the process of growth, at the same time, make sure they know that this is boot camp. It will not be easy breaking old habits and becoming disciplined. But the Commander in Chief will give them all the resources they need to become equipped to win the war.

**Know the Enemy and his Tactics.** Scripture exhorts us to be aware of the enemy's schemes, so we are not outwitted by him (*2 Corinthians 2:11; 10:3-5; Ephesians 6:10-18; 1 Peter 5:8-9*). Satan will try to deceive people into believing they are too busy to pray. He will try to instill fear of praying aloud or with other people. He will use diversions to bring distraction and confusion.

He will seek to divide and conquer by using skeptics to cause people to question your methodology.

## Have a Chain of Command.

All strategic planning must come under the guidance of the Holy Spirit. His wisdom and His command must be sought. That means that He is consulted before all endeavors. That means that prayer should permeate all aspects of the process. Listen to advice, accept instruction, and you will be wise. *Many are the plans in a man's heart, but it is the Lord's purpose that prevails. Proverbs 19:20-21 (NIV).*

## How to Prepare Others to Join

So, you've planned your strategy for an effective corporate prayer Before implementing your plan, you need to prepare the people. God, Himself provides us with the precedence for doing this. He determined His course of action and sent the prophets to tell the people what to expect. God planned salvation through Jesus, prophesied about Him throughout the Old Testament, and yet still took the time for a special season of preparation before Jesus began His ministry here on earth. John the Baptist's primary mission in life was, *"To prepare the way for the Lord," (Isaiah 40:11).* Even in salvation, rarely do people accept Jesus as Savior when they hear about Him for the first time. Before that new life sprouts within them, their hearts are prepared by the planting and watering of the seed. If God employs this measure with us to get us ready for a work He is about to do, certainly we should not skip this part of the process.

## (1) Verbally Communicate about Prayer:

- Teaching from the pulpit
- Teaching in classes and small groups
- Talking about it in one-on-one discipleship
- Suggesting or providing personal devotional books and guides on prayer
- Writing about it in the newsletter, the bulletin, or other forms of communication

## (2) Cultivate an Atmosphere Conducive to Praying:

Be devoted to prayer. Make the elements vital to this kind of atmosphere a normal part of people's experience within the body of Christ.

## (3) Show by example

The impact of modeling an effective prayer life is seen in the life of Christ. After observing the priority and passion, Jesus had in spending time with the Father, one of His disciples initiated a request to learn to pray. *One day, Jesus was praying in a certain place. When he finished, one of his disciples said to him, "Lord, teach us to pray." Luke 11:1 (NIV).*

## (4) Connect with people's motivations:

The motivation for praying, or anything we do, ought to be our love for God. Realistically, many Christians continue to be motivated more by needs, background, or personality. Connect with their existing motivations and move them toward where they ought to be. Remember that people are at various places in their walk, so a *'one size fits all'* approach probably will not work.

- For those motivated by personal achievement, help them see the benefits or results of prayer. Point them to a faithful and powerful God who will not only hear but answer their prayers.

- For those motivated by social interaction or popularity, help them see the potential of praying with others. Point them to a loving God who wants them to pray as a means of relating with Him.

- For those motivated by perfectionism and order, help them see the tools they can use to put structure into their prayer lives. Point them to a perfect and sovereign God who will answer their prayers in the right timing and in the right ways.

- For those motivated by approval or the need to please others, help them see that God is pleased when they pray. Point them to a gracious God who understands their weaknesses and helps them to pray.

Whether their motivation is right or wrong, their motivational need is what will drive them. The task at hand will be to redirect that drive on the right course. Correct motivations will come as they gain a better understanding and grow in the grace and knowledge of our Lord Jesus.

How long the preparation process will take is going to depend on where most of the group is spirituality. Obviously, everyone will not be at the same place, some will be more advanced than others. The key is to get people moving in the right direction, and when they get to where they ought to be, having a movement in place, so all they have to do is join in.

## Promoting Prayer Successfully

If everything suggested in this training is in place, then promotional gimmicks and pleading should not be necessary to get people to join the prayer ministry.

**They will Listen**

They will see that prayer is not just a passing fad but a permanent part of the church's vision. Seeing the power of prayer exhibited regularly will be certain to get their attention.

**They will put Value on it**

They will begin to see that this program is not just another program or meeting to attend, but a way of life. Eventually, they will be convinced of the benefit and priority of corporate prayer.

**They will Understand**

They will begin to see prayer modeled and not just taught. The results will impress upon them not only how to pray, but also they will begin to develop a passion for it.

**They will Act in Accordance with it**
They will begin to incorporate prayer into their own system of belief after recognizing how much it is a vital part of their relationship with God.

There are a variety of means to communicate opportunities for corporate prayer. This training allows you to have something better than any pulpit or bulletin announcement. You will have something better than a creative skit or power point presentation. You will have a viral promotion - people spurring each other on through the examples in their own lives of prayer. Use diverse types of methods of praying that will keep the motivation going.

**Prayer Ministry Growth Ideas**
Develop a prayer calendar, prayer chains, prayer cards, prayer network, prayer partners, prayer retreats, prayer concerts, prayer groups, prayer workshops, prayer journals, prayer meetings, prayer conferences, prayer lists, prayer hotline, prayer rooms, prayer rallies and organize a Prayer Summit.

# Resources

[1] Renner, Rick. The Most Common word for Prayer in the New Testament. www.renner.org/prayer/the-most-common-word-for-prayer-in-the-new-testament

[2] Strong's Concordance. http://biblehub.com/greek/4342.htm

[3] Judaism 101. http://www.jewfaq.org/prayer.htm

[4] Jewish Virtual Library. http://www.jewishvirtuallibrary.org/prayers-and-blessings

[5] Chambers, Oswald. My Utmost for His Highest (publication). https://www.utmost.org

[6] Guillermo Maldonado. Guillermo Maldonado Ministries.

[7] Thoughtco. www.thoughtco.com/columbine-massacre 1779624

[8] Procon.org. What is the Oregon Death with Dignity Act? https://euthanasia.procon.org/view.answers.php?questionID=001289

[9] California's School's New Homosexual curriculum. http://www.wnd.com/2000/12/7653/

[10] Congress.Gov https://www.congress.gov/108/plaws/publ105/PLAW-108publ105.pdf

[11] Justia, US Supreme Court, Engel v. Vitale, 370 U.S. 421 (1962) https://supreme.justia.com/cases/federal/us/370/421/case.html

[12] Player.fm https://player.fm/series/human-rights-a-day-1446196/june-17-1963-mandatory-bible-Readings

[13] Eight times the Ten Commandments had its day in Court. MSNBC. http://www.msnbc.com/msnbc/8-times-10-commandments-monument-had-its-day-court

[14] The New York Times. http://www.nytimes.com/books/98/06/14/specials/nixon-obit2.html

[15] Matthew Henry Commentary on the Bible (Concise). https://www.biblestudytools.com/commentaries/matthew-henry-concise/

[16] Blue Letter Bible. https://www.blueletterbible.org/lang/lexicon/lexicon.cfm?t=kjv&strongs=g4202

[17] Kring, A., 2017. Just the Facts 101, Textbook Key Facts. Abnormal Psychology, 12th Edition.

[18] Centers for Disease Control and Prevention. https://www.cdc.gov/nchs/fastats/emergency-department.htm

[19] International Journal of Law and Psychiatry, volume 34 (2011), pp 195-209.

[20] Go Ask Alice. http://www.goaskalice.columbia.edu/

[21] Sex Ed Enshrined in Museum with Lofty Mission. mobile.wnd.com/2002/12/16097/#l8MSOyzOOk6S7hbf.99

[22] Preces-Latinae. www.preceslatinae.org/thesaurus/Basics/Confiteor.html

[23] Judaism Stack Exchange. judaism.stackexchange.com/questions/56660/difference-between-el-and-eloah

[24] Orthodox Christian Information Center. Proper Confession and Communion. http://orthodoxinfo.com/praxis/communionprep.aspx

[25] Blue Letter Bible. www.blueletterbible.org/lang/lexicon/lexicon.cfm?t=kjv&strongs=h3045

[26] The Closer I Get to You. Written by James Mtume and Reggie Lucas. Performed by Roberta Flack and Donnie Hathaway.

[27] Blue Letter Bible. https://www.blueletterbible.org/lang/lexicon/lexicon.cfm?t=kjv&strongs=h1219

[28] Blue Letter Bible. https://www.blueletterbible.org/lang/lexicon/lexicon.cfm?t=kjv&strongs=h6186

[29] Bible Study Tools. https://www.biblestudytools.com/lexicons/greek/nas/energeo.html

[30] Bible Study Tools. https://www.biblestudytools.com/lexicons/hebrew/nas/darash.html

[31] Ask the Dreamer. http://askthedreamer.com/2015/09/04/the-ministry-of-liquid-prayers-tears/

[32] KJV Foundational Study Bible. Thomas Nelson Publishers.

[33] Bromiley, G. Theological Dictionary of the New Testament, Abridged in One Volume. (1985). William B. Eerdmans Publishing Company

[34] Ibid

[35] Bible Study Tools. https://www.biblestudytools.com/lexicons/greek/nas/axios.html

[36] Ibid

[37] Tolstoy, L. The Power of Darkness. A Word to the Wise Publishing.

[38] Hybel, B. Too Busy Not to Pray. IVP Books; 20th Anniversary Edition edition (July 31, 1988)

[39] Christian Today. 3 essential elements to the Christian's prayer life, according to Colossians 4:2-4. https://www.christiantoday.com/article/3.essential.elements.to.the.christians.prayer.life.according.to.colossians.42.4/86431.htm

# About the Author

## Evangelist Debrann Tinson

Evangelist Debrann Tinson, is a native to the country of Jamaica. She has a tremendous love for God's Word and for His people, as well as the passion for winning souls for the Kingdom. She has a contagious spirit of generosity that flows through every facet of her life.

Evangelist Tinson has been in ministry for the past thirty years, and a fulltime Evangelist for twenty years. She is an active member of Covenant Builders Ministries (CBM) in Orlando, Florida, where she is President of the Prayer Ministry along with several other responsibilities. In addition to ministering the spoken Word, she has had the opportunity to travel overseas to several different countries ministering and helping to rebuild communities. She is the founder of Prayer Warriors Seeking the Lost Ministry, where she provides food and clothing for those in need, and prays that the oppressed would be set free.

Evangelist Tinson's vision is uncompromisingly clear with one central principle; *to build and develop a kingdom of empowered people for God*. Holding firmly to the commissioned mandate in Matthew 28:18-20, *"Go ye therefore, and teach all nations"*. She endeavors to fulfill the call of God on her life to do the work of an Evangelist until the return of Jesus Christ.

She is a mother to one daughter, Sashoi, and the grandmother to Naomi.

# Notes

# Notes

# Notes

# Notes

# TO PUBLISH YOUR STORY OR BOOK

CONTACT

WILLIAMS & KING PUBLISHERS
888-645-0550
Info@WilliamsAndKingPublishers.com

OR

TO LEARN ABOUT OTHER BOOKS PUBLISHED BY

WILLIAMS & KING PUBLISHERS

VISIT

WilliamsAndKingPublishers.com

Made in United States
Cleveland, OH
17 March 2025